# Say Yes to College

For Aster.

Enjoy —

Sharon

Chandler

# Say Yes to College

## A Practical and Inspirational Guide to Raising College-Bound Kids

SHARON CHANDLER
AND ELIZABETH CRANE

Foreword by Bill Cosby

*A Perigee Book*

**THE BERKLEY PUBLISHING GROUP**
**Published by the Penguin Group**
**Penguin Group (USA) Inc.**
**375 Hudson Street, New York, New York 10014, USA**
Penguin Group (Canada), 10 Alcorn Avenue, Toronto, Ontario M4V 3B2, Canada
(a division of Pearson Penguin Canada Inc.)
Penguin Books Ltd., 80 Strand, London WC2R 0RL, England
Penguin Group Ireland, 25 St. Stephen's Green, Dublin 2, Ireland (a division of Penguin Books Ltd.)
Penguin Group (Australia), 250 Camberwell Road, Camberwell, Victoria 3124, Australia
(a division of Pearson Australia Group Pty. Ltd.)
Penguin Books India Pvt. Ltd., 11 Community Centre, Panchsheel Park, New Delhi—110 017, India
Penguin Group (NZ), Cnr. Airborne and Rosedale Roads, Albany, Auckland 1310, New Zealand
(a division of Pearson New Zealand Ltd.)
Penguin Books (South Africa) (Pty.) Ltd., 24 Sturdee Avenue, Rosebank, Johannesburg 2196, South
Africa

Penguin Books Ltd., Registered Offices: 80 Strand, London WC2R 0RL, England

This book is an original publication of The Berkley Publishing Group.

This is a work of fiction. Names, characters, places, and incidents either are the product of the author's
imagination or are used fictitiously, and any resemblance to actual persons, living or dead, business es-
tablishments, events, or locales is entirely coincidental.

PRINTING HISTORY
Perigee trade paperback edition / August 2005

This book has been cataloged by the Library of Congress

PRINTED IN THE UNITED STATES OF AMERICA

10   9   8   7   6   5   4   3   2   1

To the two most important women in my life: my mother, Shirley Bundy Turner, and my grandmother, Helen Lorene Bundy (Nanny, who lives on in my heart). I always knew that I would someday write about you to give you credit for my great childhood and for making me the person I am today. You two mothers were so good at providing for us that we kids never knew we were poor. In spite of the challenges, we always knew we had love and a place to call home. I hope you will consider this book a testimony and tribute to the strength I have witnessed and will always admire in you both. I hope I have inherited and demonstrated the same qualities in my life. Love eternally for showing me how to be a loving mother.

—SC

Many people contributed to the success of this book.

We would like to thank the terrific people at Perigee—publisher John Duff, editor Marian Lizzi, and assistant editor Laurie Cedilnik—and agent Michael Psaltis.

Thank you, Michael Bowker, for pulling us together as a book-writing team.

Thank you to Dr. Bill Cosby for allowing me to interview him thirty years ago. He gave me advice on how to treat people that I have referred to throughout my life. I thank him today for being wise enough to come to the forefront of the controversy surrounding African Americans taking responsibility for educating our children. Dr. Cosby, you are brave to say out loud what everyone already knows but is afraid to act upon. Thank you again for endorsing this book. Thanks, too, to Kim Harjo, Dr. Cosby's publicist, for her perseverance and willingness to laugh with me.

To my siblings, Gail, Dana, Jacquelyn, and Dennis, thanks for sharing your childhoods with me. Big Sis is proud of how far we have come. Love eternally for growing up with me and allowing me to develop my earliest mothering skills on you.

To my favorite aunties, Barbara and Tootsie, I wish you both could have had the opportunity to read this book. I appreciate your mentoring and support throughout my life. You will always be in my memories. Love eternally for demonstrating to me that you don't have to be the birth mother of a child to love and nurture that child. Thank you for loving me.

For my girlfriends, Georgia Lee, Ida Lane, and Synthia Smith, I appreciate your support, friendship, and experiences. As we grow older together, may we have more intelligence, patience, and humor as grandmothers than we have had as mothers.

Thanks also to my Goddess Graphics designer Suzanne Walton for teaching me the importance of presence and marketing, and to OnTrack Program Executives Madlynn Rucker and Peggy Thomas, who continue to provide me with the training, the resources and the opportunities to become a competitor in the nonprofit arena.

I appreciate my best bud, Charles Coger, for his unwavering belief in my ability to start Yes2Kollege. Thanks for all the books, computer and presentation training, nonprofit development guidance, mentoring, and most of all for your friendship.

To Richard Raucci, for reading and editing the manuscript more than once. You successfully avoided hurting anyone's feelings while making constructive comments on the structure and content of the book. Thank you.

Thank you, Philip and Michael, for your unfailing support of your mother and her all-absorbing book. You may not yet understand why the techniques in this book are important, but you will. I love you.

A special thank you goes out to both our extended families for their patience and support through the book-writing process, and to our friends who had to listen to our discussions about the book and never once asked, "Are we EVER going to be able to read it?"

And a very special thank you to Christopher and Corey for allowing me to try out on them my parenting techniques. They didn't have a choice! They have been very patient with my habit of letting the world "up in our business." I love you with all my heart. Thank you for giving me the opportunity to be the best parent I can be.

And last but certainly not least, I would like to acknowledge all the parents in my life who struggled and continue to struggle to raise intelligent, moral and responsible children, and to all the students in my life who struggled and continue to struggle to become the best they can possibly be as students and as human beings. You have my admiration and my respect. I am honored to share my stories and experiences with you.

—SC and EC

# Contents

# Foreword

Back in the day, when we were fighting for our civil rights, we understood that we had to fight for everything we needed to get ahead in this world. We understood that what was not given to us we had to take. And we did take it. We worked hard for every inch of progress for African American people in this country. But in the fifty years since those struggles, something has gotten lost. Our children are cursing and fighting each other, talking trash, dropping out, and ending up in jail. They think they're hip. They can't read; they can't write. They're laughing and giggling, and they're going nowhere. We have to do something to get our kids back on track to becoming capable, responsible, educated adults.

In lower economic areas, I'm looking at a 50 percent high school drop-out rate for African American males. I'm looking at the fact that 65 percent of incarcerated African American males are illiterate. I'm looking at 70 percent of pregnant teenagers are African American. And I'm realizing there's still a great deal of racism in this country. We take that. We all know that. But there comes a time when we have to look away from outside causes and look to ourselves to solve our own problems. This is the very essence of self-empowerment.

Self-empowerment has to do with education; it has to do with knowing English, sciences, math, and history. Education is very, very important, and it begins in the home.

First, we have to raise our children to speak properly. We are not immigrants struggling to learn English as a second language. The African American has been in this country some two hundred to three hundred years. Some families have been in places like Boston, Philadelphia, Chicago, fifty years or more. They didn't come from Europe or South America. The language that is spoken is one that is of their neighborhood. It's all right to speak it in the neighborhood, but speaking properly outside of the neighborhood will guide you toward an education that broadens your horizons. Standard English is standard English, and speaking correctly is not Black American or White American, it is American.

Studying, learning in school about the history of people on this earth—this is not "acting White." This makes you smart enough to compete in a world that, despite all our progress, may still turn against you.

It is the parents who can either encourage their child to be a better student, to achieve, or not. When a child knows that the mother or father, the foster parent, grandparent, aunt, or uncle is there for them, they behave differently. Someone is keeping on them about their homework. Someone is checking to see that the child gets to school, on time and prepared. The child knows he isn't going to be able to get away with saying, "Oh, I did my homework, yeah, it's all done." Someone is going to check. When the child knows he has to do the work, he does it.

You parents, you've got to teach. That's your job. It's not a popular job, and it's not an easy one. But you have to do it. You have to be able to say to your kid, "Turn off the TV.

I don't want you watching that." You have to be able to say, "Turn off that music. You don't need to hear that." You have to be able to say, "Get your homework done. I'll take you to the library so you can get the books you need." You have to be able to say, "Education is important in this house, and you are going to go to school and do your best."

I want you to take a pledge. Raise your right hand and swear this: I am going to be the best parent I can be. I am responsible for my children. I will raise them to be responsible, educated adults.

If you love your kids—and I know you do—you can show them that there is a different way to go, different from the neighborhood talk and the neighborhood violence. Education is their ticket to a bigger, brighter world. As a people, we can do this, but we have to make a start.

This book is a great start. Sharon Chandler's work has helped hundreds of parents and kids get on track for college. Her stories and methods have the power to make a real difference. She will give you the tools you need to get your children on the road to good citizenship and a good education. We just have to take the responsibility into our own hands and say yes to college.

Bill Cosby

# Introduction

# Aim for College

My name is Sharon Chandler. I was born and raised in St. Joseph, Missouri, the oldest daughter of a mostly single mother. We moved around a lot, but always within the orbit of my extended family: my grandmother, my aunts, my friends. I started school in the segregated South, and I finished in the first flush of desegregation. In my segregated elementary school, I was praised and petted, told I was special, told I could accomplish anything. In my integrated high school, I was told that college prep classes were not for me, that Black girls didn't go to college, and maybe I should work harder on my secretarial training. When I was growing up, college was like outer space: some place you went if you were White and you were rich.

I was told flat out that I could not go to college. I knew at the time that this wasn't true, but without the support of my school and my family, I couldn't send myself to college. I worked, I got married, I had babies. When it was my turn, I told my children from a very early age: "You are going to go to college. You have to make plans for where you are going in this life, and part of those plans involve school and higher education." They started school in kindergarten with the idea already in their heads that they would graduate not only from high school but that they would go to college.

Even the breakup of my marriage didn't distract me from the family goal of my children attending college. I moved my kids to California when my son, Chris, was fourteen and just entering high school and my daughter, Corey, was entering middle school. My new single-parent status would not be the reason my children did not achieve. If anything, they got to see their mother working twice as hard to get ahead. I worked a whole series of part-time jobs and kept the kids on track to becoming responsible, well-educated members of society.

One day not long after our move to Sacramento, I received a call from a reporter at our local newspaper telling me that my family would be featured in its Family Album column. The weekly feature highlighted the accomplishments of not-so-ordinary families in the community. The article, complete with a picture of my kids and me, talked about our higher education dreams, the obstacles we had overcome in order to get as far as we had, and our goals for the future.

A lot of people saw that article, and several of them called me wanting to know what methods I had used to raise my kids. How had I kept them focused on getting their education? How had I raised them to value their futures? Suddenly, I was handing out free advice left and right. It finally dawned on me that parents really needed the kind of information I possessed. They wanted to know the secret to how I had accomplished raising such great kids, and they were willing to take my advice. Based on the kinds of questions I was being asked, I began to create my business, Yes2Kollege Education Resources, Inc., and to develop its first and still most popular program, Six Steps to Raising College-Bound Students.

Beginning a new career is scary. I didn't take the full step from job holder to business owner for a couple of years after I started to develop my program. I worked full time as a family counseling liaison and worked on my business part time, in the evenings and on weekends. Things were slowly coming into place. I used my job experiences, contacts, and resources to help my business. When I attended workshops and committee meetings, I handed colleagues my Yes2Kollege business cards. I took advantage of trainings that benefited my Yes2Kollege business and collected information and resources that could benefit both my job and my business. I finally took the full leap to self-employment in 2003 and I haven't looked back. Yes2Kollege now offers over forty different parent education workshops and numerous classes for school-age kids, and I am busier and happier than I have ever been, helping parents help their children succeed.

## College Is an Essential Step

I am here to tell you that those educational obstacles your child faces are challenges you need to tackle together. My values may be old-fashioned ones that have been knocked about a bit, but I believe they have never really gone out of service: integrity, hard work, politeness, fairness, responsibility, family. Ideals like these are what I have built my life around, and I believe that a good education begins at home, that parents are partners in their children's education, and that the idea of college is to be instilled in children as both a right and a responsibility. My program—contained in this book—combines the values of an old-fashioned upbringing with a modern respect for education.

We all want what's best for our children. I know I did. All parents of school-age children are looking for ways to help their students succeed in school and, by extension, in life. You parents need the same things your student needs from you: positive reinforcement that you are doing a good job. You have to get it from other parents, support groups, and workshops. Now you can get it from this book.

Our education system is increasingly competitive. Just look at the rising cost of state colleges as well as private universities, and the rising SAT score minimums required for college acceptance. In order to compete in the current market, kids have to be trained to succeed. As parents, we have the responsibility to get our kids on a successful track through school and on to college.

Believe it or not, these days a high school education is hardly enough to land a job at McDonald's; without a college education a young adult is at a serious disadvantage. Minority students—my children and perhaps yours—are especially vulnerable to lower expectations, lower achievement rates, and lower employment prospects. If we want our children to succeed in this world, we have to show them that their education should be the first priority in their lives.

According to the U.S. Department of Labor, college-educated Americans are earning, on average, 76 percent more than Americans who have only a high school diploma. That number alone should motivate parents to get their kids into college!

But what exactly can you do? I talk to parents all the time in the course of my work, and they all want to know what the secret is to getting their kids focused, motivated, and achievement oriented. It's hard work, for everyone involved. I've wished and wished that I could tell them that there was a single, simple book that would help them, but there wasn't. I needed to write this book.

Family involvement in the education of children is essential to academic success. I can tell you that without hesitation. Everything I've learned—from my children, my jobs, and my own continuing education—points to this single fact. I use my own life experiences as examples of things gone right and things gone wrong, and show you ways to learn from both.

Kids need goals, and they need a quality education if they are going to succeed in life. College is not only for the privileged and the rich: It is an attainable goal for any hard-working student regardless of race or income. It is up to us, the parents, to instill in our children the awareness that college is not only an attainable goal, it is a necessary ingredient for success in the world today.

## Say Yes to College

All of these ideas have been distilled into my workshops, and now they're available in this book. My program teaches parents to have high expectations for their children from the moment they are born. By aiming for college, your student will be able to reap all of the benefits of higher education, have the ability to make a decent living, be independent, and contribute to their community.

In Part One of this book, you learn it's your responsibility to be in charge of your child and to expect obedience from that child, while enforcing rules and guidelines and teaching respect for self and others. From the day your child is born, I encourage the establishment of a home atmosphere of high expectations and family goals. I know from my experience as a parent, as a community outreach professional, and as a teacher that family support is the key to raising a successful child.

From basic limit-setting we move into the importance of establishing a lifetime love of learning and your student's first experience of school. Elementary school is the foundation for a long and successful educational career, so good study habits and parental involvement need to be well established here.

In Part Two, the middle and high school years take us through emotional changes and challenges, from peer pressure to sex and drugs. The parenting skills learned in Part One are expanded and given a workout. I'll show you how to grow your student's interests and talents and evaluate his or her potential for various careers.

While handling high school, it's time to start choosing a college. I'll teach you about the various components to qualify your student for college. Building a quality résumé, learning to write essays, meeting deadlines for testing, applying for financial aid, and utilizing your relationships with teachers and mentors greatly improve your student's chances for being accepted into the college of his or her choice. Financial aid, scholarships, savings, and grants impact the college decision-making process. You might not think so now, but you and your student *can* afford college.

Finally, after your student has left for college, it's time to make a life for yourself. Part Three is all about dealing with the impact of college separation, and enjoying your newfound freedom.

At the end of every chapter, I have provided a list that distills the ideas from that section, making it easy to refer back to the main ideas and refresh your memory of what you've learned. I call it Miss Sharon Says. Respect for elders was deeply ingrained in me. As the executive director of a community center, I was required to work with and hire older adults. I would hire senior citizens that I had said "yes, ma'am" and "no, sir" to all of my life. I was their boss, they called me Sharon and I referred to them as "Miss Laura" and "Mr. Leroy." I could never allow myself to call them by their first names. It was as though my mother, my grandmother, and all my aunts were looking over my shoulder. I was taught always to refer to adults as Mister, Miss, Uncle, or Aunt. It was a matter of basic respect. So you can call me Miss Sharon and we'll get along just fine.

Throughout my book, I will often refer to your child as "your student." Language matters. What you call someone matters. If you think of your child as a student and call your child a student, then your child will begin to think of himself as one. I drove by a local elementary school and saw on the marquee out front, "Our scholars are out of school for the summer." Scholars! This school knows what it's doing. I now refer to my workshop students as scholars. Our children are students of life, scholars in training, and I call them by their rightful name.

The best part of what saying yes to college does for parents and students is turn on the lightbulb, helping them visualize and accept the idea that college is possible for someone in their family. Most of the families I work with have never had a member even think about college, let alone attend one. I love to see that glow of hope come to their faces during my workshops and classes. I want them to change their attitudes about the possibility and the necessity of a college education. I make parents and students alike leave my classes with the mantra, "I am saying *yes* to college."

# Y2K

Yes2Kollege runs workshops and classes for students in grades three to twelve, teaching them life skills, character education, and early college-preparation skills. Students learn how to deal with peer pressure related to sex and drugs and to take responsibility for the consequences of their decisions. Lessons in integrity are incorporated in every component of the program, helping children see the importance of honesty in every decision they make and their obligations to society to tolerate and respect people and situations different from themselves.

Early college preparation gives students the skills to better organize and manage the time in their daily lives, through the use of calendars, daily planners, and diaries. Note-taking methods help students in the classroom and homework and test-taking skills help them toward better grades. Learning to become better readers is also a very important part of the Yes2Kollege mission. Discussing books that are required reading in high school prepares Yes2Kollege students early for the most important skill needed in college: the ability to understand and talk about what they read.

Simultaneously, Yes2Kollege conducts workshops with the student's parents, teaching them how to have effective parent/ teacher conferences and how to reinforce the school curriculum at home.

Most important, I stress the value of academics and good grades in early preparation for higher education. Choosing careers and researching the education needed to qualify for those careers is an important part of preparing for college. Field trips to college campuses, attending college recruitment activities at high schools, and talking with college admissions representatives about applications, financial aid, and college life are huge parts of the program. I talk to the kids about the high cost of a college education and their responsibility to help pay for it. I encourage students to save by computing how they can make a financial contribution toward their goals by saving as little as one dollar per week until the day they are accepted into a school. Yes2Kollege students research and compare college curriculums on the Internet. They also interview people in the careers they have chosen and learn the challenges and experiences of each.

All of these ideas are woven into the fabric of this book.

Every class I teach uses stories from my own life to illustrate my points. I tell the parents in my workshops and classes many of the stories I tell in this book, on how my village helped me raise my kids. I relate our experiences, the lessons we learned, the successes and the challenges, the good, the bad, and the ugly. I never say failures, because each experience teaches a lesson. If you can learn from your experiences, you can't call them failures.

While there has been progress in getting more minority kids to go to college, the number of minorities enrolled in colleges and universities is still significantly less than the number of Whites. Minority children are particularly at risk of falling through the cracks in the educational system and, despite gains in overall college attendance, are still less likely to attend college than their White counterparts.

Affirmative action is under attack on many fronts and cannot be counted on to help our children with their college admissions. I am a big fan of affirmative action, because I have learned that most of the time you have to *make* people do what is right and just, otherwise they would already be doing it. Power is a hard thing to give up. If humans were going to be fair about life, there would be no need for laws. Affirmative action was responsible for giving me my first job as a news reporter, right out of high school. Had I listened to my high school counselor, I would still be struggling to type and transcribe shorthand in order to keep a job I had no talent to do and hated with a passion. Instead, I knew that given a chance, I could learn to do anything. I applied for a job at a television station and the next day I was in the field interviewing sources and reporting on camera. In order to fill its quotas, my local TV station needed an African American face on the screen, and it also needed a female. With me, they got two for the price of one!

I finally made it to college myself too. With two kids preparing for college and all the talk at our house about where to go, which classes to take, and when to take them, it was time for me to walk the walk. I enrolled in night classes at a private college, California Academy of Merchandising, Art and Design, taking classes in interior design. This was on top of full-time work as a community outreach coordinator, and remember, I was still a single mom. I showed them if I could do it, then by God, so could they. I am pleased to report that both my children have graduated from college and both are enrolled in graduate programs. I couldn't be prouder.

When parents tell me that they will be satisfied if their student just graduates high school without getting into trouble or getting pregnant, I feel that they have given up before even starting. I encourage them to think and say, "I will be satisfied when my student graduates from his *first* four-year university." Why not?

My workshops have proven very successful. I remember one participant who showed up at several workshops. While packing up my materials one evening after another presentation, I noticed the woman walking out away from the parking lot. When I saw her outside, she was walking toward the bus stop several blocks away. She jumped at my offer of a ride home, since she was all the way across town and it was already late.

In the car, I told her I recognized her from a previous class. "Oh yes," she replied. "I go to all of your classes." She had been to seven so far! That this woman would travel all over the Sacramento area, without a car, just to hear me, blew me away.

"I needed my 'fix,'" she told me. She said she enjoyed my stories about my kids, and with all that was going on in her life she needed to hear about something uplifting, something positive and humorous that was going right for someone. She allowed as how the hassles with the bus were worth it as long as she could take home enough motivation to sustain her until my next class.

Students in one of my recent college-prep classes, fifth graders, wrote letters to me saying, "Thank you for everything, because I didn't want to go to college, but now I do," and "I know many people who don't want to go to college because they think it is a waste of time. I definitely don't agree with them." These students are no different from yours. They aren't the highest scoring or the best in their class. They are regular kids who need a goal and a push to achieve up to their potential.

I strongly believe that each and every one of us has a mission in life. I know that my mission is teaching parents and students how to prepare for a college education. I know that if I can motivate just one family to aim high by fulfilling its student's educational potential, there is no limit to the number of lives that could benefit through the ripple effect caused by that one student's achieving their college goals.

However, I am only one person, and I can only reach a limited number of people. Now it is time to take the message out to everyone who thinks that college is for someone else, or that higher education is only for the rich, or that a college education is not something their kids could ever possibly achieve. This book is my way of spreading my ideas outside of the reach of my workshops. This book communicates my core values, my methods, and my enthusiasm. Any parent can pick up on my ideas and use my tools to help their students succeed.

College is not only possible, it is necessary in today's world. Our children deserve the very best that we can offer them. College is a big step, but it is one you and your student can take if you plan for it. Using the methods in this book, you will boost your own parenting skills and inspire and motivate your children to make the most of their educational opportunities. You have to say *"yes"* to college.

# Part 1

# The Fundamentals

So much of what I teach in my parenting workshops is as much life lessons as it is go-to-college prep. The one lesson I hammer home above all others is that it is you, the parent, who makes the difference in your child's life. Choosing college means choosing involvement, at home, in the community, and in school. This book is not just about going to college, it is about being a better parent. It all starts with you.

I am a firm believer that you cannot raise an obedient, respectful child by being his best friend. And you cannot raise a college-bound student if you do not start by raising an obedient, respectful child. It all begins at the beginning. You have to start the way you intend to go on. Some people might think I'm going too far by insisting that children of preschool age can be taught to think like future scholars. But I am here to tell you, you have to build your children up from a solid foundation.

If your children are already past preschool age, don't despair. It is never too late to plant the idea in your student that he or she can go to college. It is also never too early. These lessons can be learned at any age, since they mostly involve the kinds of parenting you choose to do. I must warn you: It is the parent's involvement in the child's life that makes the difference, so be prepared to spend your time on this. The good news is you've got your very best first step here in your hands: this book. In this first section, I'll show you how I raised my children—and how you can raise yours—with respect for themselves, respect for others, and a core sense of responsibility.

# Chapter 1

# Instill Respect for

# Authority: Who's the Boss?

I started my children early on the road I wanted them to travel. I married a good man, had my babies, and set out to raise them into caring, high-achieving people. Through hard work and deep commitment, I knew my family would achieve its goals. Even though that "good man" dropped out of our lives, my commitment to my kids and our college goals never wavered.

In every workshop I teach, my students want to know how I managed it. The secret to raising obedient, well-disciplined children, I tell them, is practicing consistency with reasonable consequences. It's a lesson we as parents learn over and over through the years: it's all about appropriate limits. Establishing limits is what we as parents have to do on everything. Limits are the messages we use to communicate our rules and expectations for acceptable behavior. There are or should be limits on activities in the household, at school, or on our jobs. There are limits or boundaries on our block, in our neighborhood. There are limits or laws that govern our communities, and our societies. There are even limits to our own physical capacities. Self-limits let us know that if we do not have an aptitude for math, science, or chemistry, we should probably not bother to try to become a doctor or scientist. Limits at school might include a specific minimum or a grade point to remain in a school or get into college. Limits in our society include laws against burglarizing your neighbor's home, or laws against running a stoplight. Limits on our physical selves might be our height or weight or other physical makeup if we want to aspire to specific sports. Limits in our households might include a specific curfew, bedtime, or work or mealtimes.

In the process of raising a child we instinctively begin at the beginning, establishing limits. With a baby, the mother sets limits as to the amount of milk or food a child should have at one feeding, or even the number of times a day a child should eat. Parents limit the things a baby is allowed to touch, taste, or even see. We put plants or breakable items out of a child's reach or tell them "no" if they are in contact with something that might hurt them. The parent establishes nonverbal signals, like a raised eyebrow or frown or shake of the head to indicate disapproval. Setting limits lets our kids know that we care about them. We want to nurture and protect them from harm. And we care enough about them to want them to do their best.

Simply put, raising a child who respects limits and rules will keep him from experiencing a multitude of miseries. Rules help us show respect for the people we live with, whether in our homes, our communities, or the world. We need to know how far we can travel before we cross the state lines where laws may change and then respect those changes. We need to know how many minutes are in a quarter of a basketball game so that we know when the game is over. We need to know that the fence that separates our yard from our neighbor's yard should not be climbed or crossed, without permission to do so by that neighbor. It's all about limits.

You should not wait until a child is a teen to begin setting limits and expect that child to fall in line and not rebel against these new rules. Teaching a child to respect his body, or family members' personal property, or even household property should begin as soon as the child is able to understand. You have to be the judge of your student's developmental progress.

It is up to you to establish limits on how a child responds to your demands (such as washing the dishes, dating age, curfews, etc.) or responds to advice, especially if the child objects to the demand. Determine if negotiation is an option; keep in mind that life is not that serious, but the opportunity to teach lessons sometimes comes only once in a lifetime.

Limits answer some very basic questions. On the surface, they operate like traffic signals and provide information in the form of green lights (do that again) and red lights (stop that) for acceptable and unacceptable behaviors. Beneath the surface, however, limits answer a very different set of questions about the power and authority of the person setting the limits. Who's the boss? Who's in control? How far can I go? What happens when I go too far? The answers help children determine whether compliance with their parents' rules is optional or required. Much of what we consider to be children's misbehavior is actually limit-testing behavior or their attempts to find answers to their basic questions. Do you really mean what you are saying? How far can I go?

Don't make rules and then fail to carry out the consequences. If you do, you're sending a mixed message: The verbal message seems to say stop, but the action message says that stopping is neither expected nor required.

Don't give unclear directions. You can't just say "be good" and expect your child to know what you mean. Be clear. Attach an action to a request, like, "I want you to keep your hands away from the stove knobs."

Guidelines for stating firm limits:

- Keep the focus of your message on the behavior.

- Be direct and specific.

- Use your normal voice.

- Specify consequences if necessary.

- Support your words with actions.

The child-rearing style I teach is a healthy mix of the old way, which was my mother's style, and the new way, with some degree of understanding, compassion, and respect for my children's sense of fairness and development of their spirit. My parenting students usually respond well to the mix, since it often echoes their own, with some fresh ideas they can take home and put into practice.

When I was a child, it was understood that when our mother said something, she meant it. We never knew if it was something she had thought about or whether she was just reacting in anger, but we knew we'd better jump. If you, as the parent, get in the habit of counting to ten before you react to something your child has said or done, you will be well on the road to

# Comparison of Soft and Firm Limits

| SOFT LIMIT | FIRM LIMIT | ACTION MESSAGE |
| --- | --- | --- |
| Hitting your brother/ sister is wrong. | Stop hitting now. | Give time-out consequences to a child who hits. |
| That popsicle is dripping. | Don't eat popsicles in the living room. | Remove the popsicle from the child. |
| I just stepped on your toy again. | Pick up your toys and put them back in their box before you go outside to play. | Remove the toys for a few days if the child refuses to pick up. |
| Be home before dinner. | Be home by 5:30. | Temporarily change and shorten playtime for child who fails to be in on time. |
| I can't hear myself think! | The TV is too loud. Turn it down, please, or it will be turned off. | Turn the TV off. |
| That's not the way to play with that toy. You're going to hurt yourself. | You can play with the toy the right way or we'll have to take it away. | Remove the toy. |

saying what you mean. If you change your mind all the time, or if you give in to whining and tantrum throwing, you are no longer in charge, and no longer earning your kids' respect.

## Physical Discipline

In my workshops, the subject of discipline inevitably comes up early on. Physical punishment is an extreme consequence, but it is one of the many options we have as parents.

I learned with my kids that the rod needed administering only a few times. One such time, as every parent can relate, always happens in a store. Even after laying out the instructions before leaving home to not ask for anything (such as toys, special foods, etc.) they just had to ask anyway. Because I refused to purchase a requested item, each child, on separate occasions, fell out (threw a kicking and screaming tantrum) in the center aisle of the market. My response was an immediate swatting on the bottom and then walking away from them. I only needed to do this once for each child. From then on, our market visits were quiet, peaceful, and swift.

My kids certainly understood my approach and could communicate it to others. When Corey and I took my niece Blair and nephew Brent to Kmart, Corey instructed each, "OK, this is how it works. You don't ask Aunt Shay Shay to buy you anything in the store. If you throw a tantrum by falling out on the floor, Aunt Shay Shay will fall out with you, I'm telling you from experience!" We entered, shopped, and left Kmart with two well-disciplined kids, no fuss, no muss. Blair had a reputation for tantrums in stores, where she often tried to make her mother buy treats. With clear boundaries in place ahead of time, Blair knew that her fits would not work, so she didn't even try them with me.

Allowing a child to throw a tantrum is entirely up to the parent. There are various degrees or types of tantrums. One degree of tantrum is the actual physical screaming at the top of the lungs and falling out in the floor kicking. Another degree is the pouting or silent treatment. My take on the scenario would call for immediate attention, in the form of a spanking for the falling out and a good talking-to for the pouting episode.

A good screaming at the top of the lungs and thrashing and contorting on the floor tantrum is an excellent way for a child to express his frustrations—at home in his room, but never in public. When my workshop parents express their horror at my allowance of tantrums, I tell them that getting it all out in a safe environment is preferable to requiring a child to bottle up his emotions. Consistently suppressing the normal rages and frustrations of children can cause emotional problems later. Cooling-off time, after the tantrum has played itself out, lets the child step back from the situation and reflect on what has just transpired. It might even help him see the parent's point of view.

If a child needs a swat on the bottom after a number of requests have gone unanswered or not been acted upon, then that is a reasonable consequence. Granted, all children are not alike; they do not all possess the same temperament. Some are more rebellious and aggressive than others. You have to be the judge of what kinds of consequences suit your child.

When I was a child, most African American parents wholeheartedly believed that if you spared the rod, you would spoil the child. My mother raised five children and on numerous occasions, the rod, the switch, the extension cord, or the paddle was not spared. I believe that a lot of our discipline episodes bordered on or even crossed over into beatings. Back then, physical, emotional, and verbal abuse were all common methods for controlling children. Working full time and keeping five children safe from harm was more than you could expect from a parent.

In retrospect, I can understand the need for forceful discipline. In the fifties, sixties, and seventies there was a lot of racial tension throughout the country. In my hometown, although it was somewhat subdued, racism still accomplished its goal. We were separate but we were not equal. I feel that we, my siblings and I, were pretty insulated. We lived in an integrated neighborhood, but my elementary school was segregated. White people lived throughout the neighborhood, and we occasionally played with their kids, but there was still an unspoken rule that you stayed with your own kind. The only kind of blatant racism I remember experiencing as a child in the sixties was when I walked to the downtown library and passed little White kids playing in their front yards who would always call out, "nigger." We were instructed by our parents to respond by saying, "Your momma and daddy are niggers, so that makes you one too!" We were expected to defend ourselves with words. After a while it became a game. We would add on to the responses with any hurtful or nasty thing we could think of. The word *nigger* was used like a knife to cut out a person's self-worth; if we used it back at our tormenters we could deflect its power to hurt us.

African American parents parented the only way they knew, trying to keep their children safe while trying to promote their children's spirit. They armed us with words. While raising my kids in the eighties I fully expected my children to have this hateful word thrown in their faces, but it didn't happen. The civil rights movement had made people more aware of the damage the word could do, and it had become a word that required physical retaliation and was no longer "just a word." I could build my children's self-worth without teaching them how to cut down someone else's.

It is well known in the African American community that women during slavery intentionally emasculated their sons so as not to raise a strong, independent man. They did this in order to save boys' lives, because a strong, outspoken, protective Black male would surely be tortured, sold, or killed by the plantation master. Thank God we no longer need to suppress our children's spirits in order for them to survive.

I hear stories in my workshops about parents who are allowing their two-, three-, and four-year-olds to run the household through their tantrum-throwing antics. In my workshop for raising hard-to-discipline children I listened with tears streaming down my face as a mother related her tale of woe. She had been mandated by the courts to attend the sessions upon being released from jail because she had punched her teenaged daughter who had knocked out one of her front teeth. The mother was instructed to take her daughter back into her home to raise. Granted, I was hearing only one side of the story, but I can only imagine her frustration and fear. I hear daily of parents who have given up raising their children because they can't control them or are afraid of them. I cringe when I hear these accounts. As a parent, I refuse to feed, clothe, or shelter a child without his obedience. The only job a child has in his upbringing is to be obedient and respectful to his parents—wrong or right.

It is an even better practice to have established the rule or habit that whenever you make a demand on your child, that demand is met without explanation. When I was a child, whenever Mom called one of her children, that child did not respond with a "what" or a "yeah" but was by her side within a few seconds, before she felt so much time had elapsed that she needed to repeat your name. We knew what was expected of us, and what would happen if we didn't live up to that expectation.

I wholly believe that it is more than appropriate for a parent to expect a child to do what he is told. "Because I said so" or a request without explanation should suffice in most situations. At a workshop, one parent related his story of "because I said so" and how it probably saved his family's life. He believed in strict obedience from his children, so there were few occasions for negotiation. One night after everyone was in bed, he was awakened by noises downstairs. He and his wife, suspecting that their house was being robbed, immediately rounded up the kids by waking them quietly and signaling to them to be silent and meet in one room, as they had rehearsed in case of an emergency. As everyone obeyed his instructions without question, he was able to call the police, who arrived while the intruders were still in the house. The speaker related that had his children questioned his request to be silent and had not done as he instructed, they might have been overheard by the burglars, and there was no knowing what could have transpired then. As a result of raising children who were not allowed to question the parent's requests or argue with a decision, they did exactly as instructed in a situation where it probably saved all of their lives.

Obedience is a good thing! Children have to learn that there are rules, expectations, and laws that govern all of us, all of our lives. Whether they obey the rules of the household by performing daily chores, respecting the property of others, or trying as hard as possible to be a successful student, rules serve as a gauge for measuring good favor. Boundaries help keep order, eliminate chaos, and give everyone a sense of peace and well-being. Boundaries let us know just how far we can go, before falling off the edge. Boundaries help a child know when they are doing what is favorable or unfavorable in their parent's eyes.

When I was a child, living with my grandmother, I knew how proud she was of everything I accomplished. She would brag to her girlfriends and even to strangers who came to the house. I loved being in her good favor. As I grew to be a teenager, she never had explicit rules for me, like a curfew time, or where I could go, or with whom I could associate. But because I respected her peace of mind and wanted to always be in her good graces, I would call her to let her know what time to expect me home, I only went to places where I knew I would not get in trouble, and I associated with kids who had the same values and habits as mine. Nanny had a way of scolding me to death whenever I did something that was not to her liking. Her scoldings could last for weeks. I would sometimes wish she would just give me a good beating and get it over with!

When parents have high expectations for their children, their children will usually try their hardest to meet and exceed those expectations. That is human nature. Motivational speaker Les Brown says, "No one rises to low expectations." Expect your children to be obedient, to be responsible for their actions, and to be high achievers. Don't be surprised when they become obedient, responsible, high-achieving people.

Oddly enough, my mother often criticized me for being too lenient or permissive with my children. I would sometimes allow Chris to argue his point, or let each of them make choices for curfew time, cleaning their rooms, or even washing the dishes. I learned a long time ago that not everything needs to be done at any precise moment. My mom believed that a parent should *always* tell a child what to do, and when and how to do it. I wanted Chris and Corey to be able to think, reason, and negotiate. I didn't feel that it was usurping any of my power. It allowed them the opportunity to develop a sense of independence and responsibility.

## A Parent Can't Be a Best Friend

A parent has to make unpopular decisions and sometimes has to overrule what the children want in order to be a good parent. These are not qualities that you look for in a best friend.

The parent who has developed the ability to say no and mean it, even when he wants to say yes or eventually give in, is a parent who is not a best friend. On numerous occasions, I explained to my kids that "I am your parent. I can and will be friendly toward you, but I will not be your best friend. I am commissioned by God to protect you and love you. I am not obligated to do those things that you agree with or like in order to stay in your favor."

My husband and I seemed to always disagree about our roles as parents. The parents in my workshops have shown me that we were far from alone in our disagreement! He believed in trying to be a best friend, but I knew that someone needed to be the parent. Answer a question for me: Are you your child's best friend or his parent? You can't really be both. You're the parent! And that means you have to be able to set boundaries, teach respect, and be the one who has the final word. These are not qualities that will win your child's friendship, but it will earn you their love and respect, which are far more valuable things to have from your child. Friendship can come later.

I was usually the one to administer the discipline or the one to remind the kids about our limitations or responsibilities as parents. I remember one occasion where we were very strapped for money—utility bills can be outrageous in the Midwest, what with the freezing winters and the melt-the-sidewalks summers. We had received a shut-off notice for the gas and my husband had just received a check from his job. My son wanted a new pair of athletic shoes and had been promised he would receive a pair on the next payday. My husband purchased the shoes, even though he knew that we were scheduled to have our gas shut off. I had to be the bad guy and take back the shoes for a refund and pay the gas bill. Chris was not happy with me and my husband was furious, but parenting is about making tough decisions. It means looking out for the whole unit, not just for the individual. I love my children as much or more than the next mother, but I know that making good judgments and decisions is paramount in protecting and nurturing a family.

This kind of tough love is a two-way street. Not only is it tough on the child, it can be even tougher on the parent. Whenever I teach this section of my program, I hear groans and see plenty of eye rolling. Parents come up to me and say they don't have the time or the strength to put this into practice. It's easier, they say, to just give in and go with whatever their child wants. One woman went on and on about how uncontrollable and disrespectful her sixteen-year-old son was toward her. In the same breath, she wanted to know what type of car I thought she should purchase for his birthday! I couldn't believe my ears. My children have never been disrespectful to me and have always been high achievers, but the best I could do for them was to give my son our ten-year-old minivan for his college graduation. Why would this parent even consider rewarding her son's disrespectful behavior? Because she was still trying to be his best friend.

A car for a teenager may free up your carpooling obligations, but your obligation to teach values and responsibility should come first. You can choose to continue sacrificing your own time by transporting him wherever he wants to go. Or, you might choose to teach a lesson by declaring that you are no longer the chauffeur. Your teen must now master the public transportation system, get on his bike, or simply tell his friends that no, he can't meet them at the mall.

Tough love might also mean grounding that daughter for staying out repeatedly, past curfew, by not allowing her to go anywhere but to school for the next six weeks. After countless attempts by her to negotiate the punishment, by begging and crying, you continue to be tough by saying "no way." All attempts at wearing you down, by her begging, cajoling, wearing a long face, or her giving you the silent treatment, have gotten on your last nerve. When you have finally had enough, you say, "I will not discuss the topic beyond this point, or more time will be added to the grounding."

The point is, a lesson has to be taught to the child: You cannot disrespect my rules and be in my good favor. When my rules are dismissed or disrespected, you should expect to deal with the consequences. You always have a choice. It is up to you to be willing to pay for the consequences of those choices. This is *the rule of life.*

Take the Wimp quiz. That was tough, wasn't it? It's OK if you didn't score a zero. You can learn to do better. Kids are great manipulators. They learn early how to work their parents or whoever is responsible for administering discipline. You did it when you were a kid. I did it too. I am not proud to admit it, but I used to pit Nanny against my mother. From a very early age, I witnessed the tension in both of them when my grandmother offered any type of advice to my mother. My mom would immediately jump at the opportunity to put Nanny in her place, letting her know that "these are my kids; you need to mind your own business." Nanny would undoubtedly come back with a comment criticizing my mom's parenting skills, like she didn't feed us enough, didn't spend enough time with us, or knew nothing at all about "birthin' no babies." It's really funny, but Nanny made the same comments to me years later, about my children. My, how history repeats itself. Most of the time, when my mother and Nanny argued about us kids, my mother would lose because my grandmother was the expert at guilt. I honestly believe my mother knew what was happening, but Nanny was so good at being consistent that Mom finally just gave in. Old habits die hard. Our child-rearing habits, good and bad, transcend the generations. When we become aware of how we can act in the same negative ways, then we can begin to change. Parents come to my workshops because they recognize their own parents in themselves and they want to change.

# Are You a Wimp Around Your Children?
# Take the Wimp Quiz

Give yourself a point for each statement with which you agree.

1. I try to reason with my children when I give out consequences, but they use that as an opportunity for endless arguing, and often win.
2. My children cannot readily answer this question: "What are the rules in this house about clothes left on the floor?"
3. I often feel powerless with my kids.
4. I have to admit I'm uncomfortable when my child is unhappy because he's been deprived of something. After all, I work hard so he can have the things he wants and needs.
5. I can't follow through with consequences if it makes my child cry.
6. Sometimes I blow up after a problem has gone on too long and I give out a punishment that is too harsh. Then I let my children off the restriction before the time is up.
7. My child has such a temper that many times I'll let things slide rather than risk her blowing up at me.
8. My children don't have a lot of responsibilities around the house. I believe that childhood should be fun and carefree.
9. I try to gratify my child's every need. I don't want her growing up thinking I don't love her.
10. I want to be my child's best friend. I'd rather work things out like friends than act like some kind of boss.

## SCORING

**0–1 point:** Your kids know who's in charge. It's you.

**2–4 points:** You're a relatively firm parent, but you may want to work on being in control more consistently.

**5–7 points:** Watch out, your wimp factor is dangerously high. Sure, kids will balk at first if you strengthen your resolve. But rest assured, they *will* come around.

**8–10 points:** Your kids are running the whole show! It's time to demonstrate who's boss. They'll thank you for it—someday.

Adapted from *Raising a Responsible Child: How Parents Can Avoid Overindulgent Behavior and Nurture Healthy Children,* by Elizabeth Ellis, Ph.D. (Carol Publishing, 1995).

# Truth and Consequences

Parents have the power and the responsibility to make rules for their child's behavior. That doesn't mean that you have to become a punishment machine. Think in terms of consequences rather than punishments. When your child crosses a line that you have clearly drawn, you can remind them of the rules and give them a chance to apologize and set things right. When your child continues to cross that line (and you know they do), you actually have more choices than you might think.

First, try to remember that children are children. You were once a loud, unruly little person with limited self-control and no social skills too. Misbehavior happens. It's not the end of the world. Try to see beyond the misbehavior to the reason for it. My kids could really push my buttons, but I still tried to stop and think about how tired, bored, or hungry they might be and how that could be affecting their behavior. Understanding it doesn't really change anything, but it will soften your approach to punishment.

Natural consequences can be very effective punishments in themselves. When you get tired of reminding your son to remember to take his lunch with him when he leaves for school, inform him that it is now his responsibility to remember to take it and that you will not be running over to school to bring it to him if he forgets. A few hungry lunch hours will get the lesson into his head more firmly than all your reminders.

A change of scenery can often help a younger child break out of a misbehavior cycle. Take your child into a different room, start a different game, or sit and do something together.

This provides time and space for a talk about feelings (hers and yours) and some distance from the problem.

As your children get older, they are more attuned to the ways you say things. Instead of saying no you can offer alternatives that are really only the illusion of choice. "Would you like to brush your teeth before you get dressed, or do you want to get dressed first?" "How about we have our carrot sticks before the meal instead of with dinner?" My kids caught onto these pretty quickly, but for a while you can make that nonchoice sound a lot better than no choice. You can also practice positive language that expresses what you want without having to say "don't." Instead of saying, "Don't go in the street," say, "Stay on the grass." Once you start practicing this, you'll be amazed at how many negative commands we give our kids every day. No wonder they snap back sometimes!

Your children are under a lot of pressure to perform well, both in school and at home, but as the parent, you're under a lot of pressure too. It's OK to show your kids that you are human. You can cut them some slack on occasion by saying things like, "We can leave the dishes till morning," or "Those toys aren't going to come to harm on the floor just for tonight; I know we're all tired." I learned very early that the important stuff in the house had to be done right away, but some of the other chores? You can sometimes let the dust bunnies be.

And when all else fails and your children are making it feel like your head is just going to pop off your shoulders, take yourself out of the whole situation. Don't leave the little ones to find the matches and the knives, just go in another room or out the back door and do whatever you need to do to regain your sense of composure and good judgment. Call a friend, cry, take a shower, exercise, meditate, whatever. Do what it takes to take care of you. Because if you don't, you won't be there to take care of them.

You must keep in mind that the child is only with *you* for a few hours every day. A school-age child is unleashed on others for the remainder of the day. Other people, children as well as adults, will not think that your student is the be-all and end-all; he is just another child. He is not the smartest, cutest, or most special, not like he is to you. He has to be able to demonstrate characteristics that help make him socially acceptable so that people will enjoy, happily anticipate, and value his contributions to society.

The job of parenting can feel overwhelming on a day-to-day basis. Your child is not going to tell you every night, "Thank you, Mom, for helping me to be a better person." You have to keep working at it, without praise, and trust that the good job you're doing will pay off in the long run with children who are responsible, respectful adults.

## Miss Sharon Says

**Establish Limits:** Develop your own signals to let your child know that they've crossed over into the danger zone. This can be a raised eyebrow, a special scowl, profound silence, or just as Chris called it, a "Mommy Eye" look.

**Mean What You Say:** When stating the terms of a punishment, get out the calendar and write down the duration. Resist all efforts to shorten or commute the sentence.

**Expect Obedience:** It's OK to expect your child to do what you tell her to do. You can offer options and discuss timing, but the parent has the final say.

**Make Consequences Consistent:** Let the punishment fit the crime. Keep in mind that the child's age and the number of violations have bearing on the severity of the punishment.

# Chapter 2
# Model Respect and
# Responsibility

Children learn by doing, and they learn the most from watching others, especially their parents. If children see or hear you being disrespectful, they think this is acceptable behavior, so they repeat it. If children witness you lying or being dishonest, they will demonstrate the same traits. If children hear you curse, they will follow suit. How can you possibly demand they not curse you back?

Your actions—what you do and how you do it—are always under your child's eye. If you treat someone with disrespect, you can be sure that your child will see no reason to treat that person with respect ever again. It isn't enough for you to say to your sassy child, "You shouldn't talk to Uncle Charles that way," when you served him with sauce yourself not five minutes before. You must give respect to get respect! Respect is not gained by physical force or intimidation, but by the quality of your character.

The parents in my workshops often confuse their responsibilities or mother/father love with their right to be treated with respect by their children. I love my children with all my heart, but I would never continue to treat them with respect if it was not reciprocated. As long as a parent is parenting to the best of his or her abilities, and the child is not being neglected or abused, then that parent deserves his or her children's obedience (up to a certain age) and respect (till death do us part). As a child, I had a lot of issues with my parents, but I wouldn't dream of disrespecting either one of them, verbally or with my actions. I know they did the best they could do for me, under their limited resources and circumstances.

## Listening as a Parenting Method

All my life I have been surrounded by strong Black women who have had to single-handedly take care of their families and their communities. My mother had me when she was only sixteen. My grandmother helped raise my three sisters, one brother, and me, never complaining. She worked several jobs in the same day, cooking, cleaning, ironing, serving, and raising other people's children. From the 1950s to the 1970s, most of the Black women in my town worked as domestics in the wealthier homes, my mother included.

Between my mother's marriages starting and ending and children being born, we always seemed to end up living back with my grandmother. I especially gravitated toward my nanny; I was the oldest and felt like her favorite. I have very fond memories growing up in Nanny's house on Felix Street, with the fire station in our front door. No matter where we were living I always found myself on Friday evenings waiting on Nanny's front steps for her to come home from work so we could talk. Nanny and I would sit for hours on her front porch, rocking slowly in that iron glider with her homemade quilt-like cushions, talking about her childhood and the people she grew up with in Platte City, Missouri.

When I think about the adults who respected me enough to take the time to talk to and listen to me I remember all of those sweet and not-so-sweet old women, like Miss Allglass and her sister, Mrs. McDaniel. My favorite was Miss Magall, whose porch I sat on watching my cousins and the other neighborhood kids play while we talked about our cats. I think about my mother, who struggled with relationships, trying to give us five kids a decent father, and how no matter how bad the situation, she always kept us together and we never missed a meal. I think about my aunt Barbara, who talked to me about fashion, boys, and beauty; she gave me my first electric pressing comb and my first bottle of real perfume. She and Nanny taught me how to sew, embroider, crochet, and knit. My mom's best friend, whom we all called Aunt Tootsie, took me under her wing and showed me how to garden. She became my best friend too.

My second-grade teacher, Virginia Glass, always figures in my memories as the person whom had the highest expectations for her students. She was strict but kind, and had a genuine love for teaching. She listened when I talked about recurring nightmares and she motivated me to become a leader by giving me jobs and responsibilities in class. Listening to someone is the purest form of respect. It says to that person, "I value your thoughts, opinions, and ideas enough to give you my attention and my time." When an adult listens to a child, it can't help but build that child's self-esteem.

Working with parents, I have the opportunity to facilitate support groups where a lot of times, the parents just need someone to listen to them. Children are no different. It is so easy to bark orders at them and forget that they have ideas and opinions. I don't mean that we as parents have to argue or bargain, but we should be willing to help build their reasoning, thinking, and negotiating skills by simply listening to them.

Listening is an art. It can be powerful and fulfilling. I didn't fully appreciate just how powerful it could be until I attended a listening retreat. At this retreat, all but two of the participants were White. There was no way I would ever get up in front of this group and reveal myself. In the African American culture, it is not customary to reveal yourself to strangers (especially White folks). Until recently, African Americans would never even consider talking with a therapist (usually White) about their problems. Either the family took care of its own, or the problem was never discussed or solved. Unfortunately, most of the time the family *was* the problem. It's no wonder so many families are in need of yet more help.

During the activities at this retreat, each person was given a turn (he could participate or pass) to talk about anything he wanted. The listeners (everyone else) were not allowed to respond at all, even with "uh-huh, yeah, amen" or anything else that might distract the speaker. The speaker had everyone's undivided attention. When it was my turn, I decided I would participate, but I would only reveal things that I felt were safe in relation to the crowd. Once I began speaking, because all eyes were on me, I felt obligated to continue talking. The moderator was the only person allowed to lead or respond to the speaker's comments. She would agree with points addressed by the speaker and then gently guide you to further expound with phrases like, "You know that this has been on your mind for a long time, but now you've been given the opportunity to relieve yourself in a nonjudgmental, protected environment; it's all right to feel any way you feel." As I began giving out little tidbits of information, it became easier and felt safer to venture a little further and a little further. I felt so safe and secure in the environment that eventually I brought up feelings and experiences related to my childhood, and then feelings and experiences dealing with racism that I didn't even realize I had been holding inside. I ended up blubbering all over the place and wondering, "Where did that come from?"

All that just from the experience of being listened to. Listening is a powerful tool to use with our children. Spending time with our children, listening to their concerns without judging them, gives them the support they need and allows them the experience of expressing their feelings. Allow time daily for private talks with your children. Take advantage of the ride time in the car, or the quiet time before bedtime, or that walk to the neighborhood store, to take one of the kids with you and ask how they spent their day. I remember that Chris and I had a lot of important talks while riding from one drop-off point to another. Corey would wait until I was curled up in bed with a book, then get between the covers with me and start sighing and clearing her throat. This was her signal that she wanted to talk about something, so I would put down my book and ask her, "How ya doin'?"

In my classes for teens, the kids will come up to me and ask my advice on any subject ranging from romantic relationships to car choices to summer job opportunities. I listen to their problem without judging and then reflect the problem back to them to show that I heard their words. Not only does the student feel the respect of being listened to, he also gains the advantage of hearing his problem from someone else. I teach this method to parents as well: listen, reflect, and listen again.

This process allows your child the opportunity to reason and think out loud. You have not inflicted your opinions and your teen has been gently pushed into developing his thinking skills. You are not telling him what to do and he will feel the pride in solving the problem himself. It can sometimes be difficult to hear what your kids have to say, and it can be even more difficult to stop yourself from offering solutions, but both steps are absolutely necessary. When your child becomes a teen, your listening skills become essential for a good relationship. In most cases a teen does not want an adult always telling him what to do or how to do it. He usually wants to just get the ideas or questions out of his head and into the cosmos. He wants to hear himself think. Sometimes you will be included in this process. Your role is to listen, listen, listen.

## Pay Attention

Sometimes our kids act up because they know it will get their parent to focus on them. In order to prevent this kind of negative attention, practice positive attention instead. Special Time is a concept developed by Jean Alessi and Jan Miller that promotes many different ways to provide positive attention. Try all or any of the suggestions below and see the negative attention-getting slow down and stop.

Set aside time for one parent to spend with one child doing something they enjoy doing together. Decide together or present two or three choices from which the child can choose.

Set a regular time to do something with your child. This is a time they can look forward to, a time when they have your undivided attention. This is what they really need: just your undivided attention. Busy schedules make it difficult to spend time away from distractions, but the effort needs to be made.

Use this Special Time as a way to keep other attention-seeking behavior at bay. If your child is getting demanding about having you sit down and read a book, you can say, "That looks like a good Special Time activity. Let's do that tonight when we have our Special Time."

With younger children, this Special Time could be for short periods a few times a day. Older children may need a longer span of time, but only once a day. Schedule Special Time when you are not likely to be interrupted, and don't let interruptions (short of actual emergencies) disrupt your time together.

Family Time is great, too, but it isn't Special Time. Special Time is one-on-one. Don't fall into the trap of trying to include two children, or a spouse, in your child's Special Time.

The idea of Special Time can be expanded to include you too. Your "Special Time" might be the hour after dinner when all you want to do is sit and watch the news. If you consistently respect your child's Special Time, then you are teaching them to respect your Special Time as well.

Last but not least, don't use Special Time as a punishment or a reward. It is something you do regardless.

(Adapted from "Special Time: A Necessary but Underrated Strategy," by Frank O. Main in *The Individual Psychologist,* December 1978.)

There are plenty of ways to make the most of the time you spend with your kids. Try having a meal together (and sitting and talking longer than the five minutes it takes everyone to inhale their food) at least once a day, or have an evening every week where you take turns picking ideas out of the family activity jar (already stuffed by every member of the family) and then doing that activity, whether it's playing Monopoly or going out for ice cream. The point is to spend time together.

I always put my children in situations where they had to interact with adults. By the time they were three years old, their vocabularies were very extensive and they knew how to conduct themselves in public. Time spent with family and friends, in restaurants, at the movies, and in a wide variety of public places reinforced my message that I always expected them to behave in a way that showed their respect for the people around them, whether those people were strangers or not. People would come up to me and comment on how well behaved my children were.

My grandmother Nanny helped raise them, so I taught them how to help take care of her in her failing years. She was in their lives on a daily basis, until she passed at ninety-four years old. Even when she entered the nursing home, my children visited her several days a week. Sometimes I would leave them at the nursing home with the other patients while they attended to Nanny's grooming or pushed her wheelchair. At dinnertime, they would help feed her while talking to the other patients who were without visitors. Nanny would introduce them to everyone and tell their stories to all who would listen.

The summer Corey was ten, she would spend the mornings combing Nanny's hair and reading stories to her. One afternoon I returned to pick up Corey from her visit, when I noticed she looked ready to cry. Nanny had scolded her, telling her to never bring that book around again. "That book" was *Mufaro's Beautiful Daughters,* an African tale vividly illustrated by artist John Steptoe, and one of Corey's favorites. When Corey read it aloud, Nanny took an instant dislike to a tiny green snake in one of the illustrations, one that was all but invisible to everyone else's eyes. Corey was hurt because she had been so sure that Nanny would love this treasured book too! I explained to Corey, as fully as I felt she would understand, about Nanny's Alzheimer's disease and how it was affecting her behavior. Corey was used to her nanny being attentive and respectful of Corey's feelings. It was a hard lesson for a little girl to have to learn, but no matter what, sick or well, Nanny still loved her and needed her love and respect. Corey continued to bring in favorite books, and she tried not to take it personally whenever Nanny took a sudden dislike to something.

I encourage parents to think of everyone in their lives as a potential teacher of their children, and that there is no one they can't learn from. By learning to see what people have to offer instead of seeing only their shortcomings, we can short-circuit prejudice and teach tolerance. In my classes with school-age kids, we spend a lot of time talking about tolerance for younger kids, disabled people, different ages, other races, opinions, gender, religions, and cultures. I teach these lessons early and often because I learned them early too, and to me they are a natural extension of the self-respect I am working to get my workshop parents to instill in their children.

When I was fifteen, twice a month a couple of hundred teens met to dance the Sunday evening away. It didn't take long for the organizers to figure out that integrated dances were making everyone uncomfortable, so the dances quickly became the sole province of the Black kids, with R & B music played by local bands. Kids from all over town partied together without incident. The divisions we put ourselves in—South End, North End, and West End kids—didn't matter here. One night at a dance, Mary, a disabled girl who spoke and moved differently from the rest of the kids, asked my cousin Donnie to dance with her. He led her without hesitation onto the dance floor and danced the entire song. "I really admire you kids," one of the dance organizers said to me. "I have been coming here for several weeks now and every time Mary asks the guys to dance not one has ever refused her or made fun of her." We had all been taught to include everyone in our groups, protect them from harm, and never think we were better than a person with any kind of mental or physical difference.

Teaching our kids that not everyone looks, acts, talks, or thinks the same way we do is a big step in the direction of worldwide tolerance. I think that we Black kids were more tolerant of others because so much of the time *we* were the "others." We knew how rejection, teasing, and hatred felt, and we were taught not to inflict that pain on others. The world has lessons for all of us, and we don't always know from where they are going to come. Being open to the world and to new ideas keeps us all learning. I still teach these lessons, only now I'm teaching parents.

## It All Starts with You

If you model the way you want your child to behave, then your child will not only respect you, he will imitate your behavior. Have pride in the way you handle your business. Always be able to look yourself in the eye in the mirror and know in your heart that you did the right thing. When you make a promise, keep it. Don't lie to kids or make promises you know you can't keep. They will disrespect you and never believe your word. While raising my kids, I tried to pay a lot of attention to setting a good example and being honest, especially when I knew they would be listening or be affected. It didn't always work out that way, but at least the conscious effort was made.

All parents find occasion when they have to lie. Admit it. We lie when the bill collector calls to demand payment and we say that they are speaking to the wrong person. We lie when we tell the utility company that our payment is in the mail, but we are actually hoping for a couple of additional days to raise the money and take it to the office. We lie whenever we make promises that we know we can't keep. I remember the times in my life when I was young and adults made promises to me and were unable to keep them. I made a promise that I would never do the same to other children. It really upsets me whenever I commit and can't follow through. While raising my kids, I tried to never do anything that I would not allow them to do, or be proud of their emulating. I never lied to them, so I never tolerated their lying to me. I didn't smoke or do drugs, so I never worried about them doing those things. I was always responsible and dependable in raising them, so I raised them to be responsible and dependable to our family; I would tolerate nothing less.

Children watch and listen, even when we don't realize it. When I taught at a day-care center, I was responsible for the four-year-olds. During one of our playtimes, I observed the kids playing house. The little girl took on the responsibilities of being the mother, cooking, cleaning the house, and tending to the children. The little boy took on the responsibilities and mannerisms of being the father. He sat at the table, pretended to take out paraphernalia, and began rolling a cigarette. He chopped up the "tobacco," sprinkled it into the paper, licked the paper, and rolled it. He even went as far as to hold the "cigarette" between his thumb and index fingers, take a long draw and begin choking on the smoke. He was very adept at this procedure, so I knew that he must have watched it on countless occasions. I tell parents that they should be particularly careful when acting illegally, because kids will innocently give them away every time.

Whenever I talk with students in my classes, I always ask about their role models. They always answer with people who are in the news, who are popular in their culture, or with people like teachers who are responsible for shaping their lives in the community. I have to remind them to think of the first person in their life before a child will say that their role model is their mom or dad. It's all right for kids to want to play basketball like Michael Jordan or have the money and the possessions of their favorite celebrity. All dreams have to begin somewhere. But kids should also want to possess the morals, qualities, and values of the adult who is responsible for raising them.

When Chris was in high school, he wrote a paper in which he called me his hero. I felt so proud. I didn't realize that he had been observing the struggles and sacrifices I had made to raise and protect him and his sister. Years later, while in college, he wrote me a series of Mother's Day cards. Of course I saved them.

*Happy Mother's Day, Mom!! I want to thank you for being the strong, intelligent, determined, open-minded, selfless mother and friend you are. I also wanted to thank you and let you know that I truly and honestly appreciate all of the things you have done for Corey, myself, and our family. Without your kind heart, determination, stubbornness, and dedication to your children, we would not have made it this far. Everything we are and everything we do is a reflection of your being, your hard work, and your character.*

*I want to thank you for pushing me (never letting up) because you made me the intelligent, caring, and passionate young man I am now.*

*There is so much to be thankful for, so much to appreciate, far too much to cover here. Just know that you are loved and appreciated by your children and we hope you have a happy Mother's Day!*

It is every parent's dream to raise a child he or she can be proud of. It should also be every parent's mission to raise a child who can be proud of his parents. You need to help your child build pride in himself as well. You are your child's first and best influence. Follow these simple but powerful guidelines.

## Watch Your Words

Keep your sarcasm and critical remarks to yourself. It may be tempting to tell your child exactly how disappointed you are at their failure to accomplish something, but it is up to you to say something positive. Remember to express your disappointment in the event, not in the child. One stinging comment from a parent carries the weight of ten easily deflected zingers from friends.

## There Is Magic in a Word of Praise

Go ahead and be your child's head cheerleader. If you don't think he is fabulous, no one will, least of all him. Praise what he does and how he behaves by describing the event or selecting an aspect of the work and saying what you like about it. Be careful to praise the work or the accomplishment rather than the kid. There is a difference between, "I like the great swirls of color you put into that art project," and "You're great." The first allows the child to reflect her own self-esteem, while the second doesn't give the child any evidence on which to build a sense of self-esteem. Praise the effort, not the result. Let your student catch you bragging about him, and never diminish the value of praise by using it for everything the child does. Constantly look for ways to tell your child what you like about him. Teach your child to assert himself and to accept compliments gracefully. Accept compliments by saying thank you instead of diminishing the compliment by saying, "It was nothing." Teach how to accept failure by showing that you yourself can bounce back, and then demonstrate how to build upon the experience.

## Home as a Haven

Your child deserves to feel safe around you and in your home. Create an environment that takes your child into account by having storage space for their things and their art and pictures on the walls. Even children who don't have their own room can have their own space and have their privacy respected. Teach all family members to respect the individual's privacy and possessions. When a bedroom door is closed it means knock before entering. When the bathroom door is closed, it means that someone is using the facilities and you need to wait your turn. When a letter is addressed to an individual, it means that only the addressee should open that mail. A purse or bag belongs to an individual and not to the general public. It should not be opened by anyone other than the owner, unless given permission. Some toys are shared by the family or specific family members (such as a Game Boy, CDs, etc.). Other toys may belong only to an individual and it is up to that individual to share or not.

## Love the One You're With

Show your children some physical affection. Hugs and kisses shouldn't be reserved for when they're babies, or when they've fallen down, or only for girls. Show your spouse some affection too—show your child how to have enough self-esteem to have a loving relationship by simply *having* loving relationships with those around you. It's not just a cliché, it should be words to live by: The most important thing parents can do for their children is love one another.

Respect for property and respect for others translates well into respect for self. As far back as I can remember, I have always prided myself on being independent and able to take care of myself. Sometimes that self-confidence has worked against me, but I am always glad that I had a choice to let other people influence me or do it my way. I took that self-confidence with me through school and into my adult life, and I have tried to instill some of it in my students, both the children and the parents I teach. I always express to them the importance of having your own, no matter what it is. Whether it is having your own money, toys, clothes, car, etc., I equate ownership with power, with not being obligated to anyone.

When my kids needed new shoes, of course they wanted the one hundred and fifty dollar Nikes. I agreed to provide what I considered a reasonable $40 and they could either work for the remainder or buy something else. They always had jobs, from sixth grade through high school. They have worked for my coworkers: digging ditches, baby-sitting, entering data on company computers, painting houses, any old job they could reasonably be expected to perform. They truly know the value of a dollar. While raising them alone I experienced some guilt because I was not able to provide the extras any parent wants to give her children. But in retrospect, I know the hard times we experienced brought us closer together. They also graphically demonstrated what I was trying to teach them about the importance of a college education and how college can propel you to better jobs and a better standard of living. Without a college education myself, I was struggling to make ends meet, and they saw this and understood that I was doing my best with what I had to work with. I use these stories about my own life when I'm talking to groups of parents. There is always a roomful of parents nodding in recognition, letting me and their fellow workshop attendees know that we have all been there, and that we can all work to better our and our children's lives.

Those tough times prepare us for the real world where we have to use all of our skills and resources to get the things we want in life. As my daughter says to me quite often, "What doesn't kill me only makes me stronger." I don't need to wonder where she learned that! Like the kids of the parents in my workshops, my kids have had to do without a lot of things most others take for granted. When they turned sixteen years old, they were not given a car to drive, or even allowed to drive my car. I knew that my livelihood depended on my being able to get to work. If something happened to my transportation, I couldn't afford to make repairs; I couldn't take any chances that my teenagers would use up my gasoline or involve my car in a costly wreck. Getting an education is a great sacrifice. Gratification is delayed on a lot of fronts. Raising kids who realize that they have to work for what they want means producing adults who can take responsibility for their lives.

## Work Builds Responsibility

It can be difficult to figure out what your child is capable of doing around the house, especially since you often have to watch them moan and drag through their chores. You need to follow these guidelines to determine what responsibilities are appropriate at what age.

First, remember that you were once a child. Try to keep your expectations realistic. If you're not a model of neatness yourself, you can't expect your child to live up to neat-as-a-pin expectations. Start small and encourage task completion above task perfection. Vary the tasks—kids are easily bored—and allow a choice of jobs wherever possible. Have cleaning supplies and equipment specifically for your child: gloves, rags, spray bottle, whatever you have for yourself. And always keep in mind that these are guidelines, not rules cast in iron. You can adapt what works for you and your child from these lists.

### Five-year-old Responsibilities

Set the table for a meal, sweep the floor, plan or shop for a meal.

Tear lettuce, pour drinks, add ingredients for a recipe, make a sandwich.

Clean out the car, separate clothes for the laundry, fold clean clothes.

Scrub the tub or sink, make a bed, clean a window or mirror.

Take out the garbage.

Dress himself, tie his own shoes.

Answer the phone.

Pull weeds, prune bushes, plant plants.

### Six-year-old Responsibilities

*All of the above, plus:*

Peel vegetables, cook simple foods like hot dogs, pasta, or toast.

Prepare his own lunch.

Hang up clothes in the closet.

Water plants, rake leaves.

Walk the dog.

Wash the car.

### Seven-year-old Responsibilities

*All of the above, plus:*

Hang up towel in bathroom, leave bathroom neat.

Do simple ironing, wash floors.

Carry lunch money to school, run simple errands, bring
in the groceries.

Take phone messages and write them down.

### Eight- and Nine-year-old Responsibilities

*All of the above, plus:*

Clean up animal messes.

Begin to read recipes and cook for everyone.

Sew buttons back on clothes, repair ripped seams.

### Nine- and Ten-year-old Responsibilities

*All of the above, plus:*

Make simple recipes.

Change sheets on beds and put dirty sheets in hamper.

Operate the washer and dryer.

Shop for groceries using a list.

Cross streets unassisted.

Start to baby-sit for limited periods of time.

My children were able to cook and prepare their own meals
by the time they were about six years old. Corey used to prepare

French toast for breakfast, lunch, and dinner. She loved breaking the eggshells and stabbing the egg yolks. Needless to say, our family can now just barely stand French toast. By the time they were ten or twelve years old they could efficiently run our household, including laundry, grocery shopping, and even withdrawing money from the bank ATM to spend on household expenses. I have always had a career that required me to spend a lot of time at meetings or traveling for conferences, so I had to know that things would continue to run smoothly, even while I was away. We always had family members (great-grandmothers, grandmothers, aunts, uncles, etc.) to help whenever I was away, but a lot of the time, we didn't need to ask.

These habits of responsibility should be well ingrained by the time your child is a teenager and can be expanded as needed. As your child grows older, he should need less supervision and be given more opportunities to complete his work without being nagged. As every parent knows, however, we do have to remind our children of their responsibilities from time to time.

Chris worked for the Campbell Soup Company the summer before he left for college. I was working full time and was attending college two nights a week and all day some Saturdays. I would leave my job at 5:00 p.m. and be sitting in a classroom from 5:30 to 10:00 p.m. Chris worked till 11:00 p.m. and I was his ride home every evening, so whenever my school let out early I couldn't go home to bed because I had to go and pick him up. After he received a couple of hefty paychecks, I thought he would offer to help out with some of the household expenses, but the offer never came. Finally I discussed with him how he was now a man, making his own money, and he now had some obligations toward our home. He responded that he needed his money for "his things" and that it was my job to continue taking care of him until he shipped out for college the following fall.

Needless to say, this attitude did not set well with me. Since he wanted to be selfish and disrespect my struggle, I decided to let him struggle a little. I informed him that I would no longer put myself out, staying up late and picking him up from his job. He would now have to ride his bike to and from the job. The factory was in a pretty isolated and dark part of town and the bike ride home was, frankly, dangerous. I wasn't thrilled with the idea of him riding his bike so late at night. I worried that he would be mugged or hit by a car. In workshops where I tell this story, parents come up to me later and always comment in fear and disbelief about this portion of my talk. How could I force my baby into such a dangerous position? I knew he needed to experience a little hardship in order to appreciate the sacrifice I had been making by picking him up in my car.

Most of the parents tell me that they would never have done this, but I tell them that sometimes extreme measures will get results. The fact that I, too, was suffering a little hardship here, worrying about my baby, meant that this situation needed to be resolved quickly. After two days of him riding his bike, I instructed Chris to leave $250 on my pillow by the time I returned home from work the following day, or he could try to find room and board somewhere else for that amount or less. The next evening, there was the $250 on my pillow, and an apology besides.

That summer Chris and I both learned a lesson. I taught him that he had a financial responsibility to his family. I had worked several jobs to keep him safe and secure over the years. We were a family with obligations to each other. He also had an obligation to me—I was paying all of my income keeping a roof over his head and food in his stomach, which, as any mother of a teenage boy will tell you, is no small feat. At that time, I was not receiving child support so every penny I made went toward the rent, utilities, car payment, and all the household expenses, food, clothing, and entertainment teens require. I love my children with all of my heart, but I will not let them abuse, misuse, disrespect, or pimp me. I have feelings too!

Kids have to be *continuously* taught to be considerate, responsible, and respectful. I thought that Chris would automatically offer to help out with the bills, but he didn't see where my responsibilities toward his living conditions were waning and where his were beginning. I had to explain my reasons for wanting help and he had to recognize that by paying his own way he would exhibit to me that he was ready to become a man and accept responsibility for himself.

I could have easily said, "OK, I'll continue to foot all of the bills. He needs all of his money to buy clothes and things to get started in school in the fall. It's only for a couple more months." I realized that my mother or my husband's mother would have reacted by letting Chris's behavior slide. But I had vowed never to raise my son to be irresponsible or disrespectful to women, like so many of the men I know. My mother complained that I treat Chris different than I treat Corey because he is adopted. I know I treated them differently because of their gender, not their natural parentage, but I love them equally. It is a treatment issue, not a love issue. With Chris I raised a man, a man I am proud of and respect on so many levels. He is kind, gentle, responsible, loving, intelligent, honest, and respectful, to name only a few of his attributes. He is a beautiful man. Not a boy in a man's body. He is not in denial of his shortcomings, but works on his strengths. I am so proud to be his mother and he knows it.

The safe and happy resolution of this period in Chris's life always gets a big sigh of relief from my audiences! Chris is attending law school and married to a lovely young lady. He continues to be a loving and supportive brother and son. I let him live his life, but he knows I am always concerned about him. He supports me by sending me cards to pick me up and calling to let me know that he loves me and respects my struggle. He is a great son, a loving son, a man.

## Miss Sharon Says

**Listen to Your Kids:** Time yourself in a conversation and see how long you can go before interrupting, interjecting, or making judgments. Listening is a skill you have to practice.

**Expose Your Kids to Other Adults:** Take your kids with you when you volunteer in your community. Let them participate and experience the joy of giving.

**Be the Person You Want Your Kids to Be:** Let your kids see you in situations where you stand up for yourself, even if it's awkward. Stand up to bullying, be patient with the disabled, speak up against racist or intolerant speech.

**Build Self-Esteem Through Responsibility:** Start with small tasks and be sure to praise all efforts. Make it clear that the whole family has responsibilities to one another.

# Chapter 3

# Set the Stage for

# a Lifetime of Learning

What I call life skills are just as important as the three Rs your student learns at school. As I teach in my workshops, life skills include reading, but they are also about relating well to others, effective communication, and organizing your time. The willingness to learn is the most important single skill we can teach our children. In order to do that, they have to have curiosity and a desire to know more than they are being told. Parents in my workshops are brought up short at the notion that their video game–playing, I-don't-care-about-anything child can become an inquisitive, knowledge-seeking person, but I can tell them confidently that it is possible.

The same is true for parents. Parents who are themselves lifelong learners—who read, take classes, and are involved in the community—demonstrate to their kids the importance of being in the know at any and every age.

I have always valued the power of education. My kids heard from both their father and me how important it is to continue to learn, even outside of school. I had a clear idea, very early on, of how I wanted to raise my children. I've changed as my children have grown, but I never wavered in my core beliefs, that children should be obedient, thoughtful, and encouraged by their parents to do everything that furthers their education. Learning and accomplishment are never ending, and the process of learning is an ability that everyone possesses. It is school and so much more.

## Speak Up

I've always maintained that the Black community needs to foster a bilingual population. I'm not talking about taking Spanish or French—that's a different issue—and I certainly don't advocate Ebonics. I mean that all our children should learn that there are times and places where it is appropriate to speak in a certain way, and times and places where it is appropriate to speak another way. Speaking correct, grammatical English is a necessary ingredient for success in this world. No one will take you seriously if you *sound* uneducated, even if you have a dozen diplomas hanging on the wall.

Parents tell me that their children don't want to speak well because the kids complain they get teased for sounding White or trying to sound better than their peers. I tell parents that our children can become chameleons of language, changing the way they speak depending on the situations. As children, my siblings and I could always tell when my mother was speaking on the phone to a bill collector or a businessperson. Her voice would get softer, more cultured, and more correct. We all knew to be quiet when my mother was speaking, but we were silent as the grave when she spoke that way on the phone. To us, she sounded like a different person. As soon as she hung up and said something ordinary, she returned to the person we knew.

We all do this, sometimes unconsciously. We speak with our friends and relatives in a slangy way, saying "she gone" and "I ain't" and the like, and then turn around and say to a stranger on the phone, "My mother isn't available to come to the phone right now. May I take a message?" Teaching our kids the difference is important in the long run.

The language we use speaks volumes about who we are. If we use slang and profanity in our daily lives, we are displaying an ignorance of standard English that, in my life, is unacceptable. There is absolutely nothing wrong with having higher standards. "It's hard," I told my kids, "and you won't always be popular, but you have to stand up for what you believe in."

All of my life, Blacks have made fun of me because I am articulate. Although I did not do well in English in school, I always had a good sense of what sounded correct when spoken. I spoke Standard English, even in the company of my peers. Of course I also spoke the current slang, but only when I was in a relaxed atmosphere, like on the playground, at a friend's house, or at home. We are all bilingual to some extent, but there is a place and time for everything.

I never thought I was "acting White" by speaking correctly. I was simply speaking in a socially acceptable language that everyone could understand. Early on, I realized the power that language possessed, especially where adults were concerned.

As a kid I remember knocking on strangers' doors and selling Christmas cards. I had quite a lucrative business. I also competed in church oratorical competitions. I had no way of knowing then that those experiences were preparing me for a career in public relations, communications, and eventually writing.

In my classroom, no one is allowed to swear or use "the n-word." My students understand that I will not disrespect them with racial slurs and they will not disrespect me in the same way. I explain to my young students the history and the mission of the word *nigger*. Its mission has been and will always be to demean and dehumanize Black people. It has worked its magic for more than four hundred years—in that amount of time it has become a powerful weapon. How can Black people casually accept a new interpretation of the meaning of the word?

Throughout our history in this country, Blacks have engaged in and been victims of fights, riots, and even murder because of those two syllables. Now I hear kids of all races calling each other by that name. They don't understand what they are saying because no one has explained to them the history.

I remember when Chris was a teen and I overheard him and one of his best friends, Greg (a White boy), in a conversation about an event at school. Greg was excitedly talking about their other acquaintances, saying n-word this and n-word that. I could not believe Chris could take part in this conversation without telling Greg it wasn't cool to say that word and he'd better shut up. When I called Chris aside later, he explained that it was just a word, it didn't mean anything anymore, it was just a figure of speech. "Everybody says it now," he told me.

"You're not everybody," I snapped back. "And Greg doesn't know what he's saying." I explained the possible ramifications of his allowing Greg to say that word. He could be overheard by a Black adult who has strong feelings and a history with the word, and how Chris might be injured trying to support and protect his friend if there was an altercation. I further explained that the word is dangerous and it still accomplishes its mission to hurt and destroy the self-esteem of Black people. I don't know what Chris told Greg, but I do know that I never heard Greg say that word again in front of me.

When we call each other the n-word or allow our children to use the word, we fail to honor the memories of the Blacks who risked their lives meeting and planning in basements, churches and caves to found the more than two hundred historic Black colleges because they were not allowed to get an education with everyone else. We show disrespect for our family members whose dreams of getting an education were quashed because they had to support the family by waiting tables on railroad cars, raising other peoples' babies while leaving their own with other family members, cleaning and serving Whites in homes they couldn't even dream of living in, let alone someday own. We make a mockery of the sacrifices of the minds and bodies of our forefathers and mothers who spent fifteen-hour days in fields picking cotton and tobacco or crops of healthy food they were not allowed to eat. Our history in this country is one of suffering and triumph, and the word *nigger* belongs to that history. It has no place in anyone's daily vocabulary.

I had a parent in one of my workshops question my insistence that they should teach their children to speak without slang. I countered that it was easy to learn how to speak sloppily and that any child will learn it from the children and adults around them, but from their parent they should learn how to speak well. To this day, I can hear my kids automatically switch from talking in a way that, if I didn't know them, would make me think they'd never been to school in their lives, to speaking like they'd swallowed a grammar book. The world is a wide place, and to get along in it, our children need to speak many languages.

## Read All About It

Nothing opens us up to language and the world like books. When I was in sixth grade I had Miss Shirley Krump, a teacher whose assigned topic was instructing us on the history of Europe and Asia. Her enthusiasm for the subject just about matched ours—we were practically comatose for most of the class period—so one day very early on in the semester she suddenly dropped into her desk chair and announced, "Let's read a story."

She pulled out a hardcover copy of *Charlotte's Web*. I'd never heard of it. But once she started to read, I was enthralled. She didn't just read, she acted out the story with different voices for the animal characters and thrilling pauses at all the exciting bits. I was transported to that farm and cared deeply about what would happen to Charlotte, Wilbur, and Fern.

I'd never had anyone read to me like that, and from the rapt expressions and open mouths around me, my classmates never had either. All these little Black kids who had never been read to were suddenly introduced to the classics of children's literature. Miss Krump knew she had touched a deep chord in her class and from then on would take any opportunity she could to read to us. She talked to us about books as though they were friends, friends she couldn't wait to have us get to know. I began going to the library two or three times a week, even though it was a mile and a half walk each way over a hill. I checked out all the books Miss Krump read to us, and then began to check out others that caught my attention. When she read us *A Wrinkle in Time,* I thought I had discovered a whole new world. In a way, I had. Miss Krump made books and stories important to me, and I shall always remember her fondly for that.

My mom, though she didn't read to me, demonstrated a devotion to books that I didn't appreciate until I was much older. I can't remember a day growing up where she didn't have a book in her hand. She constantly purchased and traded novels with friends and used bookstores. She amazed me with the speed at which she was able to finish a book. One day she was reading about the love interest of some ingénue traveling to a foreign country and the next day she was starting a book about the mistreatment of slaves on southern plantations. Her example has snuck up on me as an adult; I rarely find myself without something to read. Your student shouldn't have to wait for a Miss Krump to come along and inspire him. You as the parent have all the tools you need to get your student to read.

But why is everyone always carping on reading? Reading Is Fundamental is the name of a huge nonprofit children's literacy organization. Reading is always being pushed as the single most important accomplishment your student needs to master. Reading this, reading that, reading, reading, reading. We all get tired of hearing about reading. Beyond the obvious notion that everyone needs to be able to read street signs, tax forms, and grocery receipts, why is reading so important?

Reading is the one skill that your student must master in order to be able to study *any* other subject. He can't progress through school without being able to read a science text, learn from a social studies handout, or understand all the words in a math problem. Encourage your student to read anything he can get his hands on. When you think about it, probably 95 percent of going to college is about being able to read and then comprehend what you have read. I love reading and try to keep at least three books open under my bed where I can read a chapter from each one every night. I don't think it matters that much what a student reads as long as he enjoys it. We all have different tastes and interests, so try not to discourage or tease a child who loves to read comic books instead of Great American Novels. Show interest in whatever he is reading by asking him to explain the parts you don't understand. Communicating by critiquing stories or books is one way to open the door to trust and respect. Relating stories and characters to your everyday world can be fun and a learning experience for you as well.

Early success in reading is directly linked to later school success. Statistics show that if a child is not reading at grade level by third grade, then by fifth grade it is almost too late to catch up. Before third grade, your student is learning to read; after third grade, he is reading to learn. Without that understanding of what words mean and how they go together in a story, your student is at a serious disadvantage for the rest of his school career. You need to do everything you can to develop your student into a reader.

Like anything else, your student will want to read if he thinks it's fun. Reading shouldn't be a chore or a punishment. I used to tell Chris, "Go to your room," as a punishment, but I would also add, "Go to your room and read a book." I wanted him to sit quietly and reflect on why he was being punished. Later, I started to notice that while Corey was interested in books, Chris never voluntarily picked up and read anything. It finally dawned on me that he associated reading with punishment! I immediately stopped punishing him by making him read and started encouraging more reading for fun. Children who read for pleasure are reinforcing their reading and comprehension skills and entertaining themselves at the same time. So raise a reader. Read to your student from their earliest days. Have books, magazines, and newspapers in your house, and let your student see you reading them. Even bath time can be book time: Plastic books designed to get wet make great reading in the tub.

Little habits can mean a lot. Establish DEAR times (Drop Everything and Read) where everyone in the house has to stop what he or she is doing and read a book. Read aloud, even after your children can read for themselves.

Be a regular visitor at your local library, but don't stop there. Start your own library. I always gave books as presents to my children, nieces, and nephews—friends too. Sharing a favorite book is a way of sharing a piece of yourself. And having that book on the shelf, watching a book collection grow, taking care of books, lending them out, and trading them for others are all ways we can keep our ties to books. I know brand-new books can be expensive, but book collecting doesn't have to be. New paperbacks are always cheaper than hardcover books. Libraries have sales of their discarded books, books at thrift stores are cheap, and there are many used bookstores across the country; you just have to look for them. Garage sales are also a great source of books, especially since you can often buy an entire collection or series of books for a song.

You can also make your own books. I'm not talking about writing the Great American Novel; I mean a book of photos or of cutouts from a magazine. Books without words are a great way for younger children to "read" you a book. Corey made a little book that was all pictures of desserts cut out of magazines and glued onto paper. It even had shiny foil candy wrappers on the last page. She "read" that book over and over. A book that shows your son as a baby and then as a toddler and then as a big boy will, I guarantee you, be thumbed endlessly. As your kids get older, encourage them to write stories and create books of words and pictures they've made.

None of these suggestions are foolproof—you could do all these things and end up with a student who can read but who doesn't really like it. When Chris showed signs of hating reading in seventh grade, his teacher and I devised a way to entice him back into books. I found books that had to do with famous athletes, books of startling science facts, and books of riddles, all things I knew he would want to hear about if the information was on TV. Once he got excited about the subject, he became more willing to pick up the book. That and the fact that the television was off during the school week put him back on a book lover's road. I also had a weekend bedtime reading rule: He could stay up late one night as long as he was reading in bed. It was a struggle, but with time and patience, Chris got back into books. Now, as an adult, he subsists on a steady diet of luxury car magazines and law books. At least he's still reading!

If your student is a reluctant reader, use her interests, movies, travel, and art activities to spark connections to books. Books based on popular movies—and movies based on books—are everywhere. Books about places you've visited or places your child wants to visit are a way to explore without leaving your house. Books that involve a game or a do-it-yourself element can also motivate a reluctant reader. From lift-the-flap books to choose-your-own-ending young adult novels, nothing grabs a kid's attention like a little interactivity.

I always used to love to share what I was reading with my kids. I would read out loud the parts I thought were funny, or important, or stupid, from whatever I was reading that day. Chris and Corey got in the habit of doing the same thing. It doesn't mean the same if you can't share it with somebody. Even though they're no longer in the house, I'm always sending them titles of the books I'm reading and suggesting they read them too. I love it when I get clippings from the newspaper in Chicago where Corey is now in school. She'll scribble a note across the top that reads, "I read this and I thought you'd like it too."

While you're at it, teach your student how to use reference books like the dictionary, thesaurus, and encyclopedia. I know the Internet is taking over, but a good grounding in reference techniques will stand a student in good stead, and fewer and fewer schools bother to teach library skills anymore. If you yourself don't know, then ask your librarian for help. That's what she's there for!

To tell if a book is at your child's reading level, use this rule of thumb: Have your child read a page of the book aloud. For every word she doesn't know, she holds up a finger. If, after a whole page, she holds up all four fingers and the thumb, then that book is probably too hard for her to read on her own (though it still might be a good read-aloud book). Early reader books often have a number on the front

Black families can hook a reader with stories about the Black experience. Here are my suggestions from a reading list designed for college-bound students:

**Agee, James**
*A Death in the Family*
The story of loss and heartbreak felt when a young father dies.

**Angelou, Maya**
*And Still I Rise*
Poems reflecting themes from her autobiography.

**Anderson, Sherwood**
*Winesburg, Ohio*
A collection of short stories lays bare the life of a small town in the Midwest.

**Baldwin, James**
*Go Tell It on the Mountain*
Semiautobiographical novel about a fourteen-year-old Black youth's religious conversion.

**Brooks, Gwendolyn**
*Selected Poems*
Poetry focusing on the lives of African American residents of northern urban ghettos, particularly women.

**Delany, Sara and A. Elizabeth with Amy Hill Hearth**
*Having Our Say: The Delany Sisters' First 100 Years*
Two daughters of former slaves tell their stories of fighting racial and gender prejudice during the twentieth century.

**Ellison, Ralph**
*Invisible Man*
A Black man's search for himself as an individual and as a member of his race and his society.

**Gaines, Ernest**
*The Autobiography of Miss Jane Pittman*
In her 100 years, Miss Jane Pittman experiences it all, from slavery to the civil rights movement.

**Giovanni, Nikki**
*My House*
The poems in this collection deal with love, family, nature, friends, music, aloneness, blackness, and Africa.

**Haley, Alex**
*Roots*
Traces Haley's search for the history of his family, from Africa through the era of slavery to the twentieth century.

**Hurston, Zora Neale**
*Their Eyes Were Watching God*
Janie repudiates many roles in her quest for self-fulfillment.

**King, Martin Luther Jr.**
*A Testament of Hope: The Essential Writings of Martin Luther King, Jr.*
King's most important writings are gathered together in one source.

**Kotlowitz, Alex**
*There Are No Children Here: The Story of Two Boys Growing Up in the Other America*
Lafayette and Pharaoh Rivers and their family struggle to survive in one of Chicago's worst housing projects.

**Lee, Harper**
*To Kill a Mockingbird*
At great peril to himself and his children, lawyer Atticus Finch defends an African American man accused of raping a White woman in a small Alabama town.

**Malcolm X, with Alex Haley**
*The Autobiography of Malcolm X*
Traces the transformation of a controversial Black Muslim figure from street hustler to religious and national leader.

**Mills, Kay**
*This Little Light of Mine: The Life of Fannie Lou Hamer*
Fannie Lou Hamer, a sharecropper's daughter, uses her considerable courage and singing talent to become a leader in the civil rights movement.

**Morrison, Toni**
*Sula*
The lifelong friendship of two women becomes strained when one causes the other's husband to abandon her.

**Paton, Alan**
*Cry, the Beloved Country*
A country Zulu pastor searches for his sick sister in Johannesburg, and discovers that she has become a prostitute and his son a murderer.

**Parks, Gordon**
*The Learning Tree*
A fictional study of a Black family in a small Kansas town in the 1920s.

**Walker, Alice**
*The Color Purple*
A young woman sees herself as property until another woman teaches her to value herself.

**Wright, Richard**
*Native Son*
Bigger Thomas, a young man from the Chicago slums, lashes out against a hostile society by committing two murders.

of the book, indicating which reading level it is appropriate for. Again, your librarian can help you find books at your child's reading level.

## Go Out and *Do*

But they can't get everything they need from reading about a subject—they have to go places and see things in order to grasp the full impact of history or current events. We have to expose our kids to all kinds of experiences. On a trip sponsored by the National Association for the Advancement of Colored People (NAACP), nine-year-old Corey and her grandma, my mother-in-law, met Ms. Rosa Parks, the woman who helped launch the civil rights movement when she refused to give up her seat on a bus, December 1, 1955, in Montgomery, Alabama. The theme of the weeklong convention was "The Struggle Continues," with more than twenty thousand delegates converging on Detroit from all across the country.

Corey and her grandma listened to Reverend Jesse Jackson speak about the importance of education and to Benjamin Hooks, former president of the NAACP, speak about civil rights and a recent Supreme Court decision regarding discrimination in the workplace. This was also Corey's first airplane ride. Our local newspaper interviewed Corey and her grandmother upon their return, and Corey was quoted as saying that she thought Ms. Parks was nice but old like her grandmothers.

My mother-in-law took my kids on a four-day round trip from Missouri to Washington, D.C., so they could all attend an NAACP commemorative march. She purchased NAACP memberships for each of them and had them participate in the march because she wanted them to understand and experience firsthand the history of our struggles.

I asked my kids what they considered the best part of the trip to Washington, thinking they would remark on the thousands of people they saw, seeing the nation's capital, marching in a huge crowd, being in the presence of famous people, etc. To my surprise, they thought the best part of the trip was eating at all of the interesting truck stops. You can never tell what children will get out of an experience. At least the food was good!

I never worried that my children wouldn't be able to travel with another adult, or that they would embarrass themselves (or their parents) in public. They knew how to behave and how to speak. All you hear from the media is that kids are dangerous, kids are bad. Seldom do they run a story about the kids who make good grades, help in community development volunteer programs or are working after school to help support their families. The hype is usually negative and at some point we all, as adults and media consumers, buy into it. I've been guilty of believing those lies myself.

## Manners Matter

On a day that had presented more challenges than usual, I had one more stop to make before I could go home, put my feet up, and forget all about my workday. That last stop was a delivery of my educational program materials to the principal at a local inner-city elementary school. As I approached the door, my arms loaded down with a large box full of materials, the dismissal bell rang. I almost panicked as I imagined the doors in front of me bursting open. I knew the rush of students making their way off campus would trample me. I had a clear picture in my head of the onslaught of bodies that would knock me to the ground, trample my box and me, and then run away as though nothing had happened.

Instead, to my surprise, a tiny little boy who could not have been older than five met me at the door. He held the door open and stepped aside to let me in. I was amazed at his manners, especially since that image of a herd of unruly children was still clear in my mind.

"Thank you so much for holding the door for me," I told him.

"You're welcome, ma'am," he responded, and then he was gone.

I stood there for a moment, shaking my head at my mental picture of what I had thought these kids were going to do to me. My box and I made our way to the office, where I made a point of telling this story to the office secretary, all about my expectations, my surprise, and my renewed trust that young people can be taught to be caring individuals. I also asked her to pass the compliment on to the school staff and to the parents of that little boy for helping to raise such a well-mannered young man.

I had let the hype get to me. I had gone into that school with low expectations for it and for the students it produced. I know I was wrong, and I hereby apologize. That inner-city school has high expectations for its students, despite what the world might see as a losing situation. The teachers, staff, and parents are definitely raising students who reflect well on the community that raised them.

I equate polite speech with good manners in general, and I never underestimate the power of good manners. The good manners of one little boy changed my attitude about his entire school. If you do no more than teach your child how to say "please," "thank you," "yes, ma'am," "no, sir," and "excuse me" when appropriate, then you have already done a great deal. Having good manners teaches our children to treat others as equals who deserve the same common courtesy that they do. Having good manners is more than behaving well in public; it is about feeling empathy for other people. I warned you that my values are old-fashioned; you can't get much more basic than the Golden Rule: Do unto others as you would have them do unto you. Don't knock it; it works.

## It *Does* Take a Village to Raise a Child

At nearly every workshop I lead, parents complain that the village has disappeared, that people no longer want to help each other, and that close family is no longer close. Nowadays, the village doesn't come to you; you have to work to create a village around you and your children. The village in my community has consisted of aunts, uncles, cousins, friends, neighbors, and strangers from my neighborhood, jobs, schools, and church, and I am always adding new members. My friends joke that I know everyone in town, and I have to confess, it sometimes seems like that to me too.

In the African American community, the village is particularly powerful. It can make you or break you. It can uplift, nurture, promote, motivate, support, and love you. Or it can accelerate the negative talk, the opinions about you and squash all of your hopes and dreams. I have been fortunate; the village has usually been in my corner. Throughout my lifetime, the village has helped build and nurture my self-esteem by allowing me to lead it in civil rights demonstrations, recommending me for jobs, allowing me to serve as its spokesperson dealing with the Environmental Protection Agency (EPA), and working with me to develop social service and housing programs to help the community. I gave to the village and the village gave right back to me. I expected it to be there for me because I had always been there for it, and it didn't let me down.

When my then-husband, Thomas, and I were looking for a home to purchase, back in the late seventies, we took several things into consideration. First, of course, was affordable monthly payments, but a close second to that was, is it close to relatives for when we had children? And finally, was it within walking distance of schools? A small Victorian in my midwestern town only cost us $8,000 for a two-bedroom bungalow in an upper-lower-class neighborhood. The house was built in the late 1800s and its original owners had passed it down to their only son, who sold it to us. Even better, my husband had been raised right next door.

The house was ideal, located only four blocks from an elementary school. I envisioned my kids walking to school with the neighborhood kids, attending all of the special events at the school along with my neighbors, and being able to drop in on our kids and see how they were getting on in school.

Two years after moving into our new neighborhood, we adopted Chris as a newborn. Two years later, Corey was born and Chris was ready to attend preschool. Life was busy with babies, school, and work, but we were all well and happy, working on our goals. When both kids were of school age and learning well at our local school, Everett Elementary, the boom was lowered. We were notified that the school was going to close. I immediately began organizing the community, meeting with neighbors and community leaders to develop a plan of action against the closing. We met almost daily to research how this could be happening and what actions we could take to reverse the decision. We organized petition drives, spoke before neighborhood groups, and marched in picket lines before each of the school district board members' homes.

Nothing we did had any impact on the school closure. Maintenance on the building had been deferred for years. It was too late to make repairs or renovations economically feasible. The district had redesigned the school boundaries, thus decreasing the number of children enrolled at the school. The district could then make the argument that the school no longer served its community and that the projected number of kids available for enrollment was insufficient to support the school in the future. It closed.

It just wasn't fair that the school board could take away our school. We had to let them know we were here and that we were angry. There were lessons to teach our children, our politicians, and our community. Our village was coming apart and we had to do what we could to repair it. One of the most valuable lessons we can teach our children is that life is not fair. No matter how wrong, unfair, or unjust something might be, it can still happen to you. The school closing was unfair to all of the children who had attended that school. It was unfair to every family who had, like me, moved into the neighborhood with the expectation of being able to send their children to the neighborhood school. It was unfair because now, those children would be bused out of their neighborhood to communities that were not necessarily accepting of them. Those children who were previously involved in extracurricular activities after school (such as sports, clubs, etc.) would now be excluded, because they would now have to leave school when the bus was ready to leave. Few had access to any other transportation.

It took time, energy, and money, but we impressed upon the school district that they would have hell to pay, coming into our neighborhoods and closing any other schools. We showed them they weren't dealing with passive, ignorant constituents. As a result of all the school closure fights, I decided to run for a school district seat. I didn't win, but I was in the running, and the experience charged me up even further to remain involved in city politics. Another community advocate who cochaired our committee meetings with me ran for city council, and won! We now had a representative—who just happened to live around the corner from me—looking out for our concerns on a grand scale. We didn't win the school closing fight, but we were winning the war. Some years following the school closing, a school district representative told me that the school superintendent had vowed never to close another school in our neighborhood without first consulting the community. We set a precedent and put in place a system for future neighborhood activism. I take great pride in what we accomplished.

The whole ordeal taught our community that although we were economically challenged, living literally on the other side of the tracks, we still had a voice that had to be considered. We were homeowners and voters in our community, giving us as much credibility and power as our more affluent neighbors. We were empowered to begin attending the school board and city council meetings and to set up neighborhood organizations to review our findings concerning our community. We began meeting regularly with our city council member, who educated us on the working of city government.

I tell parents that you can't sit back and simply allow the village to take care of itself. You have to build and nurture your village. Every society has its worker bees, and if you are one of them, you are placing yourself in the position to benefit from the village you work to create.

The school closing affected our neighborhood in ways that we could never have imagined. As a result of the closing, a large part of our sense of attachment to our neighborhood disappeared. Parents used to meet to nurture and support each other's kids at school recitals or at sporting events. We would brag about our kid's accomplishments over the backyard fence. We would discipline each other's kids as they played stickball in the street. We would meet at each other's kitchen tables to complain about the lack of public transportation in our neighborhood or get excited about the proposed opening of a new department store in the mall. Our kids were now bused out of our neighborhood according to the space available in other schools. Within a three-block radius of our home, kids attended four different schools.

The mothers who met during the Christmas holidays in each other's kitchens to bake cookies for the school bake sale never met again. We didn't know what our kids were doing in school because we stopped attending school meetings, where we now felt uncomfortable or left out. We couldn't attend recitals and sports events because we couldn't get to the school during work hours and because we didn't necessarily have transportation to get there during our off-hours. Our kids didn't know each other. They no longer played together or even talked to each other. The neighborhood games of hide-and-seek, jump rope, and dodgeball ceased. It was like someone had taken the heart out of the neighborhood. I felt that the neighborhood had died and the hopes we had for our kids enjoying all of the benefits and joys their father and I had experienced in a loving, close-knit environment as kids—and that we had fostered when our school was in our neighborhood—would never again be experienced by our own children.

When I was growing up, my siblings and I knew that our actions were under the close scrutiny of every adult on the block. We would meet the wrath of Miss Loretta or her husband Old Dude if we cursed or didn't play street games by the rules. Miss Rosie would treat good kids to an afternoon of watching *American Bandstand* or *The Mickey Mouse Club* on her new television. The firemen across the street would allow obedient, respectful kids to tour the fire station with newly acquired friends, or treat their neighborhood favorites to a free soda pop on hot summer afternoons. In an emergency, our neighbor Miss Snookie could be depended on to remove a bean from my baby sister's nose, when my parents left me in charge as baby-sitter.

Various neighbors could be enticed on a Friday payday to purchase ice-cream cones for everyone from the Jolly Roger's truck. Those same neighbors would tell your parents about your brother lighting a fire in the dilapidated doghouse, now serving as the neighborhood clubhouse, with matches stolen from your kitchen. Those same firemen would assist you countless times by rescuing your cowardly cat from the front-yard catalpa tree, or provide relief from the heat by opening the corner fire hydrant.

Like all parents, we wanted our kids to have at least what we had enjoyed or better. We wanted our kids to perform skits and dance routines together, while we oohed and aahed from our front porches, with our friends from the neighborhood. We wanted our kids on hot summer nights to catch lightning bugs and put them in jars. We wanted our kids to learn how to repair their bikes from the neighborhood handyman down the street. We wanted our kids to be able to hang out with other adults and kids, who we knew and trusted, after school at the neighborhood community center. And we wanted our kids to feel loved and protected by their neighbors and responsible for their community.

Because of our struggle, my family and community learned valuable lessons about working within the system to effect change. If you are on the outside looking in, complaining and criticizing, you can't do squat. You have to be willing to stand up for your convictions and *work from the inside*. My community and family learned that you have to pick your battles and go in with realistic expectations so you can experience a realistic sense of accomplishment. We need to teach our children that you take small successes and build on them or you can take losses and disappointments and regroup with new strategies. I remember the words of Don McCrary, a White minister from my hometown, while speaking to the African American community during a commemorative march celebrating the birth of Dr. Martin Luther King Jr. saying, "Never let anyone tell you they are looking out for your interests. You have to be equipped and prepared to look out for yourself." I have never forgotten those words, and I repeat them to every roomful of parents I address. We have to be willing to commit to a cause, do the best we can, pray on it, and work with the results, good or bad. My neighborhood—my village that I had worked so hard to foster—never really recovered from the school closing, but it did survive.

## What If Father or Mother Doesn't Know Best?

Parents in my workshops worry that they have to be the source of everything for their students. Many of us haven't graduated from college ourselves, so we think we can't inspire someone else to want to learn. Nothing could be further from the truth! It's not only OK to say you don't know something, it's actually a good thing. You're a human being, not a machine, and you can demonstrate that to your student. You have neither an endless supply of patience, nor an endless supply of information. You can, however, still answer those questions. The trick is to know how to find the information.

- Your public library. Your public library is there for you, and your librarian is simply dying to look up the answers to your student's questions.

- Your home library. If you collect books, especially books of information, you can always say, "I don't know but I can look it up." Consider getting a set of encyclopedias.

- The Internet. A home computer is much more than a game machine. With an Internet connection, you have instant access to online libraries, published articles, and tons of other information. It's worth the expense.

- Your village. If you don't know the answer, you might know someone who does. And your kids might be more willing to listen to someone else tell them things, anyway.

# Village 101

You can create your own village in any setting. In Sacramento, my local coffee shop has become my village meeting place. Since my kids have moved out, I don't have school as an obvious cornerstone of my village, but colleagues, neighbors, and the folks who sell me coffee all qualify as villagers. Sometimes it really is as simple as the *Cheers* song makes it: What you need is a place where everybody knows your name.

To make everyone feel like a member of the village, call everyone by their name. When you call someone by name you are acknowledging him or her as an individual. You are saying, "I know you, I see you," and, by extension, "You are important to me." Kids, especially in their teenage years, use the adults around them to reflect their own ideas of who they are. A name embodies who a person is and becomes a powerful statement of identity. Use kids' names, say hello to them, even when they are ducking their heads and trying to avoid your notice. Don't humiliate them, just say hello.

There are any number of things you can do to create a village around you and your family. Here are just a few that I recommend in my workshops: Host a block party, join a church, talk to your neighbors, create a community garden, paint the houses of senior citizens on your block, engrave identifying marks on kids' bikes (to aid in their recovery if stolen), or invite law enforcement reps to neighborhood meetings for property and personal safety tips. Your village also consists of the political representatives in your community. There are always opportunities to make them feel more responsive and responsible toward your village. You could invite them to the neighborhood barbecues or clean-up parties or visit them at their offices to let them know how you feel about the job they are doing. Just look in your phone book in the City and County section. These are your public servants so use them. They work for you. Be the kind of person people want to know. Pretty soon you'll have an expanding network of friends and acquaintances who will support you and who, in turn, you will support.

I mercilessly use my kids' lives to illustrate the points in my program. Chris and Corey have had to get used to everyone in my classes knowing their business, but I find that parents relate well to my real-life examples, so I continue to tell all. A few years ago, my village rallied to help me keep Corey in her private college. Corey's first year at college was a difficult one for her. She has always been a very introverted person, shy, quiet, and private. Her whole high school life she had only two friends. She told me that was all she needed. When she moved into the St. Mary's College dorms I knew she would have a difficult time making friends, but I hoped she would at least participate in the campus activities and make a couple of friends. She ended up coming home almost every weekend, sitting in front of the TV watching sports and hanging out with me. I knew I would have to do something different the following year.

I explained that in her second year she could come home only once a month. She took it personally, of course, but I tried to explain that she was doing herself a disservice by not becoming involved in the campus activities. She called me one afternoon to inform me that she was going to apply to the University of California, Davis, which her brother was attending. Her reason was that she didn't like St. Mary's and she had now decided that a large university setting was what she really wanted. She had chosen the private college because of the classroom size, the isolated location, and the fact that she felt she didn't want to get swallowed up in a campus of twenty-five thousand.

I began working the village to support my reasons for her staying at St. Mary's. First, I needed information from people who understood Corey's situation. At the time, I was working with a lady who taught English at California State University, Sacramento. I told her about our dilemma and she strongly suggested that Corey stay where she was. She agreed that Corey selected a private college for all of the right reasons and that she should give it more time before deciding to move away. I also talked with several graduates of St. Mary's who also said that Corey should try to make it work because she would eventually realize the advantages of a smaller school. I even brought up the subject with grocery store clerks and fellow commuters, anyone who could give me a fresh perspective. I enlisted everyone's aid—friends, colleagues, experts, even total strangers—in supporting me and my efforts to keep Corey where she was.

All my work paid off. Two months after returning to school, Corey informed me that she had been invited by one of her professors to participate in the exchange students program to University of Cape Town in South Africa. She was thrilled. This opportunity changed her entire outlook on college life, gave her something to look forward to, something to work toward, and a reason to love her school. She could now go on to become a fully realized member of her college.

The village not only strengthened my arguments about her staying at St. Mary's, but it also settled my mind and quieted those uncertainties I had concerning my advice for her remaining where she was. I had never advised anyone about a similar problem and in the back of my mind, I wasn't always sure I was giving her the best advice. I told my village what I needed, and it responded.

So despite the fact that my kids complain that I tell everything, I continue to talk about what we need and try to help others with the information I have been blessed to learn. I believe when we share our blessings with others it makes room for us to receive more blessings. I have been helping people my entire life. Although some things have been difficult, my skills and abilities to network with others have been priceless for my family and me. I have received so much help and support and useful information from strangers who are willing to share their knowledge and expertise. The village and I have always had a very satisfying and mutually beneficial relationship. *If you are willing to support your village, it will support you right back.* And if you don't let others know about your dreams, those dreams will never become your realities.

Even today, I continue taking classes in fine art, parenting, workshop presentation skills, public speaking, teaching youth, or managing a business. I truly believe that learning is a lifetime commitment. It amazes me to think that the length of time I have been on this earth—and what I have been able to learn while I have been here—is still like a single grain of sand on a vast beach of knowledge. There is always something new to learn. That is why I encourage everyone to continue attending school, to take advantage of every opportunity afforded them, and never to feel that they know everything. God will humble you in a heartbeat.

# Miss Sharon Says

**Reading Matters:** Subscribe to the newspaper. Get magazines into the house. You can read any newspaper in the world on the Internet. Just read!

**Experience the World:** Travel with your kids whenever possible, near or far. Let your kids plan trips by researching places of interest.

**Organize Your Time:** Keep a calendar of important family dates and events for everyone to refer to.

**Fight to Protect Your Village:** Join your neighborhood organization. Vote in city, county, state, and national elections. Know the candidates and issues. Your voice counts.

**Remember Names:** When you meet a new person, repeat their name back to them after they say it. This will help cement it in your memory so you can then use it every time you see that person.

# Chapter 4

# Elementary School:

# The Foundation for

# Academic Success

Before your student ever went to school, you were his first teacher. If you value education, achievement, and learning, then your student will too. You are not only your student's first teacher; you are her *best* teacher, and your involvement in her formal education means the world to her. In order to convey that commitment to education, you have to be involved in the life of the school.

I always quote former vice president Al Gore in my workshops. "We have to have parent involvement to raise successful kids," he said. "The most promising approach to improving our schools may be the oldest and most obvious: getting families more involved in their children's education."

So be involved! Get to know your student's teacher, keep up with the classwork and curriculum, attend school events, and know what is expected of your student. Encourage enrollment in cultural events, extracurricular activities, and math and science enrichment. Even at this tender age, your student can learn the benefits of volunteering and building a network of supportive teachers, administrators, and community leaders.

I know from hearing countless parents tell me they don't have time that there is a real gap between parental work hours and school volunteer hours. You're busy. We're all busy. Regardless, I still tell parents, your student's school needs you, and your student needs you at school. Do what it takes to put in the time.

Showing your "face in the place" sends the message to the school and to your children that school is important to you and the family. A lot of times my then-husband and I were unable to attend events, but we always sent snacks or money to help with supplies. Sometimes we would take a lunch hour and spend it in the school cafeteria instead of at work.

I was always invited to read to Corey's class during Black History Month. One of my favorite books to read was *Stevie* by John Steptoe. Steptoe, an African American author who went on to write many highly acclaimed children's books, wrote and illustrated this book about two African American boys when he himself was still a teenager, so I always used that fact as a way to get the kids to understand that the author of a book could be someone a lot like them and not so very much older. *Stevie* tells the story of an only child, Robert, whose mother takes in a younger boy, Stevie, while his mother is starting a new job. Robert is understandably jealous and behaves in ways that every child I've ever read this story to can understand. It's a story about sibling rivalry, plain and simple, but it is told with such heart and sensitivity that I have read it over and over again and can continue to feel for Robert, Stevie, and their mothers.

I read *Stevie* to Corey's sixth-grade class one year, and when they saw the book they all started grumbling that I was reading them a "baby" story and that they were too old for picture books. But when the story started they hushed right up and listened. They may have thought they were too old, but *Stevie* spoke right to them. In the discussion afterward, Corey tried to act embarrassed as I used our family stories to help make Steptoe's story come to life for her class. I know she didn't stay embarrassed for long because she always asked me back to read.

## Know Your Rights

Teachers and school administrators have to understand and be sensitive to the attitudes and ideas parents of color have toward the education system. Until the 1960s, this country's education system was not inclusive of African Americans. Parents and grandparents of students in our schools right now have had past negative experiences in the educational system and tend to bring those memories with them in dealing with current administrators. I feel it is the school's responsibility to develop opportunities to partner with parents, helping them set family education goals for the student. When the family, school, and community nurture and support a child who wants to succeed, it's very difficult for him to fail.

Stumped for what to do at your child's school? Try any or all of the following:

Join the PTA.

Bake for a bake sale, or help plan one.

Act as a lunchroom or playground monitor.

Chaperone field trips or any events that take place away from school.

Help plan and chaperone dances, proms, or graduation ceremonies.

Act as a classroom helper, or volunteer in the computer lab.

Organize or assist with a club or special interest group.

Help out with the gym or sports activities.

Help prepare press releases or write grant applications.

Work in the library.

Sew costumes or build sets for theatrical productions.

Help out with any arts, crafts, or design projects.

When all ideas abandon you, ask your child's teacher!

Many parents take their participation in their child's school for granted. A mom in my Raising Successful Students workshop went on and on about how important it was for her kids to have her at school and actively involved. I looked at her and shook my head. While I congratulated her on her involvement, I found it amazing that she took it so for granted that all she had to do was show up and the teachers and administrators would welcome her with open arms. It isn't like that for many Black parents. In fact, her comments struck me hard as being just the opposite of the experience of most African American parents in their interactions with the education system. In many cases Black parents are not welcomed in the schools. They are not encouraged to volunteer to help with projects or to even inquire about the progress of their child until that child is having serious problems. Most parents of any color don't know that they have the right to be included in the educational process and to have access to the system on behalf of their children, period.

I am here to tell you, you have the right to observe your student's class, read your student's file, and have regular meetings with your student's teacher. You have the right to know what is going on in school. You have the right and the responsibility to request that your student be tested—academically or psychologically—when it is clear there is some reason she is not performing up to grade level in her schoolwork or her behavior.

## Attending a Parent Conference

Before you even set foot in the classroom, take a minute to prepare. First, talk to your student. Ask what she would like you to discuss with her teacher, and if she has any likes and dislikes about how the class spends its days. Then promise (and this is important) that you will talk to her after the conference and let her know what was said.

Take some time with your own thoughts before your conference. Prepare some questions in advance. For instance, you

In California, your rights are outlined in Chapter 864, Statutes of 1998 Education Code Sections 51100–51102 as the following rights of parents:

- Classroom Observing: To visit their child's classroom to observe activities. The time and date of the visitation must be arranged in advance with the school.

- Teacher Conferencing: To request a conference with the child's teacher(s) or the principal. Contact the school to schedule a convenient time for all participants.

- Volunteering: To volunteer their time and resources for the improvement of school facilities and programs. Contact the school to determine the terms and conditions of this service.

- Student Attendance: To be notified in a timely manner if their child is absent from school without permission.

- Student Testing: To be notified of their child's performance on standardized and statewide tests and the school's ranking on these tests. (Under other state law, parents may request that their child not participate in the statewide tests.)

- School Selection: To request that their child be enrolled in any school in the district. The district is not compelled to grant the request.

- Safe School Environment: To have the assurance of a safe and supportive learning environment for their child.

- Curriculum Materials: To examine the curriculum materials of the class or classes in which their child is enrolled.

- Student Academic Progress: To be informed of their child's academic progress in school and of the persons to contact if they wish more information or assistance with their child.

- Student Records: To access their child's records and to question anything they feel is inaccurate or misleading or an invasion of privacy. Parents have the right to a timely response from the school district about their questions.

- Standards: To receive information regarding the academic standards their child is expected to meet.

- School Rules: To receive written notification of school rules, attendance policies, dress codes, and procedures for school visitations.

- Psychological Testing: To receive information on all psychological testing recommended for their child.

- Councils and Committees: To participate as a member of a parent advisory committee, school site council, or site-based management leadership team in accordance with established rules and regulations for membership.

Do a little research with your state or your school district to determine if they have a similar "Bill of Rights" for parents. If not, you need to work with your school administration to begin the process to adopt a set of rules that work for your school.

might want to know if your student has any learning disabilities, whether she is working at grade level, or whether she is above grade level. Find out if your student is more often a ringleader or follower when it comes to class projects. Is she disruptive or generally obedient? Make sure you ask what *you* can do to help her at home to be more successful at school.

Her teacher will want to know if your student has any medical needs, any favorite subjects or hobbies, and/or whether anything particularly stressful is happening at home that could affect her school performance (a new baby, a move, etc.).

While you are at the conference, ask to see your student's work—the teacher will no doubt already have prepared a whole folder for you to look at. If the teacher talks about something you don't understand, don't be afraid to ask for explanations. Teaching, like any profession, has its own terminology and shorthand with which you might not be familiar. Before you leave the conference, go over what has been said and whatever agreements you may have made so that both you and the teacher are clear on any plan of action.

After the conference, you still need to follow up. Have that talk that you promised your daughter, relating to her what was said and agreed on at the conference. Stress anything positive that was mentioned, and talk about suggestions for improvements. Together with your child, make a plan to carry out those improvements. Make sure you review progress reports and report cards whenever they come home.

## Special Education, Special Considerations

When Corey was in first grade, I knew something was wrong, because she never wanted to go to school. She had loved kindergarten and had always cheerfully left the house for school. Now, every morning, like clockwork, Corey would develop a stomachache, headache, or some other malady that could possibly warrant her staying home from school. My grandmother baby-sat Corey and Chris from the time they were born, so Corey knew that if she didn't go to school she would be spending the day with Nanny. After a while, I began to get curious, especially when she reported one morning, "Mommy, I can't go to school today because I'm sick."

"What's hurting you today?" I responded on cue.

"My arthritis is acting up today, I think I'd better stay home."

When I asked her how long she had suffered from arthritis, she claimed to have caught it from Nanny.

I didn't bother to explain to her that arthritis is not contagious and is very rare in six-year-old girls. I instead made an appointment to visit her school. Something was seriously wrong and I was determined to get to the root of whatever it was. I asked to look at Corey's papers and her grades. I was so disappointed to learn that she had never passed a spelling test and her classroom assignments were incomplete.

"What is going on here? Corey is failing everything!" I exclaimed in disbelief. It was only the second month of first grade, but my bright little girl was so far behind it seemed impossible that she could catch up. I know that students learn at different rates and at different times, but I was looking at evidence that—at school, at least—she was just not getting any of it. This six-year-old child who took my telephone messages, kept track of everything that was needed in the household, and who had an advanced vocabulary, was a very poor student.

I went to her teacher and insisted, "I want her tested so we know how to help her."

"I felt that Corey was having problems," her teacher admitted, "but I didn't want to be the one to suggest that she be tested . . ." She never finished the statement, but I knew she wanted to say, "Because she is Black." I knew that Black kids were being placed in special ed classes in many schools, but

I didn't care right then about the other kids. I wanted to get whatever help was needed for my child. I didn't care about the stigma or the stereotypes about Black kids in special ed. I cared about helping this intelligent girl over whatever disability she had so she would enjoy school and not look for excuses not to attend. I understood the teacher's dilemma. She felt we would be offended by the mere suggestion that Corey might have a disability, so she chose to ignore it rather than take a chance of insulting us.

Black children are nearly three times more likely than Whites to be labeled as mentally retarded, and nearly twice as likely to be labeled emotionally disturbed. In the 1998–1999 school year, more than 2.2 million children of color in U.S. schools were served by special education. Among high school youth with disabilities, about 75 percent of African Americans, compared to 39 percent of Whites, are still not employed three to five years out of school, according to the Civil Rights Project at Harvard University and the National Center for Education Statistics.

Following a couple of days of testing, it was determined that Corey had a reading disability called dysgraphia. Dysgraphia is a learning disability that affects writing abilities. It can manifest itself as difficulties with spelling, poor handwriting, and trouble putting thoughts on paper. At that time, Corey was having great difficulty printing. A lot of her letters were unrecognizable and often written backward. She had a terrible time reading and spelling words. Even though she was only in the first grade, she had been reading for a while. I thought that as soon as she started attending "real school," not kindergarten, she would better acquire the skills she needed to progress in these areas.

Corey immediately began the extra classes for the last forty-five minutes of the school day. I really appreciated the sensitivity the teachers displayed for the students' feelings. Special ed kids didn't know they were special ed kids. They just knew that they got more time in the computer lab than everyone else. Special ed teachers introduced her to software programs designed to strengthen memorization and eye/hand coordination. This process helped her spelling. Our family purchased a computer and I daily made her type out each word on her list ten times, which helped her memorize the words for the weekly spelling bee. I also began reading to her—and with her—more often. We spent long hours reading to each other curled up under the covers of my bed. I would read a page and she would read the next.

In our home, reading books became a big affair. We no longer purchased a lot of toys as gifts for Christmas or birthdays. We now looked for storybooks and books of poetry. We scouted garage sales for whole collections of fairy tales and for the comic books Chris loved.

Corey spent the next four years in special ed classes, but by the fifth grade, she and I read *To Kill a Mockingbird* together and had begun critiquing Stephen King novels. When we moved to Sacramento, Corey was beginning sixth grade and she no longer needed the learning disability classes. She was doing so well academically that every year from that point on, she was on the principal's list for academic achievement. In college, she consistently made the dean's list and graduated with honors. She still experiences difficulties spelling, but thanks to spell-check she does just fine.

As I always tell parents, with any problem your student is facing, the most important element to helping them eliminate or learn to work with it is having patience and being encouraging. By praising the student for her hard work, you reinforce the adage that "practice makes perfect."

If your student needs special attention for a learning difficulty, it is great that our school systems have help available, but be aware that some schools have disproportionate numbers of Black children—especially Black males—enrolled in special education. Do some research on your school and school district. Ask questions and ask for data on the racial population and other children qualified for special ed classes. Learn how your school disciplines "hard to control" children. Does it use special ed as a disciplinary tool? Who is making the recommendation that your student be placed in special ed? What are their qualifications? Ask to speak with other parents of children with disabilities, so you can compare notes on their challenges in this area. When working with school staff to develop a plan of action for your student (an Individualized Education Plan, or IEP), be armed with some knowledge of the laws and where your student stands in the process. The Internet has a wealth of information on this subject, with Web sites answering learning disability questions from parents and kids.

Once your student is placed in special ed, ask how long she will need to remain there. Ask what your family can do at home to help her with her disability. Read, research, and ask questions. And above all, you must schedule monthly or quarterly meetings with teachers and administrators to discuss and monitor your student's progress. Notice I said *you* schedule regular meetings. This is your child; she is counting on you to help her through her disability.

# Good Study Habits Make Great Students

Have a regular time and place for doing homework. Insist that your student bring homework home daily. If homework isn't coming home, you need to follow up with the school to make sure that none has been sent home. Make yourself available for homework assistance and offer other resources if needed. Tutoring in a particular subject can be arranged whether through school or on your own. Keep a list of people and phone numbers who can assist with school assignments. Is Aunt Maxine a whiz at math? Can Neighbor Joe be relied on for untangling tricky writing assignments? Check and make sure they're willing to help, and then add them to your Specialist Homework Help List.

You can make a homework zone in your house, even if it's a corner of a room with a desk and a lamp. Having a specific place to do homework assists concentration. You can also get in the habit of asking questions before and after a homework session to find out what needs to be done and then to make sure it has gotten done. It's not your job to do the work for your student, but you can and should point out what hasn't been done and what has been done incorrectly. Don't forget to praise a job well done!

Even when they don't have homework, homework time should be spent reading, not watching TV. Never have the TV on while they're doing homework, even if it means you have to miss something *you* wanted to watch. It's more important to limit the number of distractions so your student can focus on homework.

A study from the Henry J. Kaiser Family Foundation from October 2003 showed that children are watching more television than ever, and they're watching at younger and younger ages. Among children under two, a whopping 59 percent watch TV every day. On average, kids zero to six spend two hours a day in front of some kind of media—that's TV, computers, videos, and DVDs. That's a lot! I know it's convenient to keep the little ones entertained while you get dinner on the table or while you do something else, but what message are they getting? You need to use television judiciously and set limits on what they watch and how much. When you can, watch with them and then discuss with them what you've seen.

These kinds of discussions don't have to be limited to TV topics, though that can be a good place to start. Home was your student's first learning environment, and it should continue to be a place where learning happens. Talk about school, talk about what your student is learning. If you're following the advice in this book, you have plenty of reading material you can discuss. The point is to keep the conversation going and to keep learning happening.

## Miss Sharon Says

**Show Up at School:** Offer your special skills to your student's teacher. An ability to sew, fold origami, draw, or act can spark opportunities for you in your student's classroom.

**Know Your Rights:** But respect the rights of the school administration as well. They are working with you, not against you.

**Move Through and Beyond Special Ed:** Special education is not a dead end for your student, nor is it something to be ashamed of. Use it to help your child, then get past it.

**Just Do It:** Weekend homework doesn't have to be done last thing Sunday night. Establish Friday night homework sessions so the weekend can be spent relaxing and recharging for the coming week.

# Part 2

## Making the Grade:

## The Crucial Middle School

## and High School Years

Middle school is a pivotal time in your student's life. You might want to ignore puberty and keep your baby a little longer, but the hormones bubbling in your preteen will not be denied. This age is a time of big changes for your student, and you as the parent are going to have to keep up. If you haven't been there in elementary school, you can still make the effort in middle school. It's never too late to get involved at your student's school.

The same holds true for high school. If you've done your homework, high school isn't such a scary place. And if you've followed the guidelines in this book, you've done your homework. Now it's the home stretch. Continue to do all the things you've done in middle and elementary school—you've laid the groundwork for good studentship—but it's time now to add a few higher expectations.

Parents tend to pull back when their kids reach high school, and stop volunteering in school. Parental involvement in kindergarten is usually pretty high. By the time your cute little five-year-old is a gangly fifteen-year-old, it's likely you'll be too busy or too intimidated to volunteer in school or even to show up for school events. There seems to be some sort of un-written rule that as students get older they need their parents less. It's not true. They might not want you to be sitting in their class cutting out construction paper flowers for an art project, but they still need you to know what's happening at school, to sign permission slips and drive for field trips, to send in pizza for the class party, and to show up for teacher confer-ences. You have to stay involved.

# Chapter 5

# Middle School:

# New Challenges,

# New Solutions

When Chris started middle school, I attended an orientation for incoming parents where I was handed a flyer called, "Easing Your Child's Transition to Middle School." I hand it out now myself in my parenting classes for the parents of middle schoolers. It includes many of the themes in this book: Keep track of your student's homework, spend time together, know their friends. But the biggest message in that handout—and the biggest challenge—boils down to staying involved in your student's life and in the life of the school. Even when your preteen is acting out, pushing you away, and giving you a face full of attitude, they are still in just as much need of you as they always have been. Even though their adolescent attitude might put you off, you have to continue to participate at and around school.

When Chris was in the seventh grade, he had to write a report about mummies. A mummy exhibit featuring the Egyptian child pharaoh King Tutankhamen was running at Chicago's Field Museum. In an effort to give Chris an opportunity to make a really great report, Thomas and I decided to spend a long weekend in Chicago. We loaded up the family car, enlisted the participation of a few friends and their car too, and traveled the eight hours to Chicago.

We thought that finding a motel in Chicago would be a cinch. Wrong. This particular weekend was the first time ever that the Rolling Stones were performing in Chicago. We couldn't find a place to sleep anywhere. After several hours of looking, we happened upon a hotel in the heart of the city, one with plenty of rooms. That should have been an indication that something was wrong. After checking in at the desk and unloading all ten people's bags from the two cars, we opened the doors to our rooms and turned on the lights. Roaches dropped from the ceilings and ran across the beds as they scurried for cover. Stay here? *Sleep* here? No way.

After collecting our money from the front desk, we decided to spend the night in our cars. Ten people, spending the night on the streets of Chicago. The following day we contacted a relative of one of the friends we had brought along, and fortunately he let us spend the night in sleeping bags on his living room floor. The kids thought the roaches, the driving around not knowing where we would spend the night, and the sleeping bags on the floor were enough to make the trip memorable. But we weren't done yet.

The next day, our host treated us all to a fish fry at his restaurant in a seedy part of downtown Chicago, an area I would never have taken them otherwise, and it was by far the best fish any of us had ever had. We rode the El from one end of Chicago to the other, just so we could say we'd taken the El. Of course, we spent an entire day at the Field Museum getting an eyeful (and a notebook full) of information for Chris's report on King Tut and Egyptian mummies in general. On the way home, the kids pestered the adults to find out when we could all return to Chicago and do the whole trip again. They loved every minute of it. To this day, they all still refer to the trip as "the time we were homeless in Chicago." And, Chris received an A on his report. This story always gets a great response in my workshops.

I'm not suggesting that you have to drive across the country every time your student has a report to write. You can find and use resources closer to home. The point is to understand what is needed and help to provide it. These habits, like good study habits, are important to establish early, so when your student hits high school the homework demon will be easier to tame.

Other factors contribute to school success as well. Get your student to school on time and encourage regular attendance. Make sure you all get enough sleep. The best school in the world can do nothing with your student if he or she is not in a seat, alert and ready to learn.

I have to bring up again how important it is to make sure your student is reading at least up to his grade level. You need to continue to stress the importance of reading by continuing all those great reading habits you started when they were

113

younger. Hang out at the library, develop your home library, and let your student catch you reading.

## Don't Dumb Yourself Down

Somehow the Black community has made the association between being well spoken and educated and "acting White." This drives me crazy. Having enough respect for yourself not to use slang and profanity means you are a strong, educated person with a future and a place in this world. Remaining ignorant of the wider world and what it takes to be successful in it keeps our people down. In my view, there is no such thing as "acting White"; there is only being educated, and that does not make you anything other than yourself.

One of my sixth-grade students asked me, "Is it true, if you're smart, when you go to middle school you get beat up every day?" This is a reality—our students feel unsafe in school because they are high achieving and willing to learn. School should be the place where learning is prized, the place where a display of intelligence should be recognized, nurtured, and celebrated. That our students are made to feel small by being called smart makes no sense to me. But the message a students gets from his adolescent peers is clear: If you continue striving to be a good student, you will have to fight for your life every day. A whole lot is wrong with this picture.

African American students are as intelligent—even more intelligent in some cases—than the school population at large, but because of their peers' jealousy and ignorance, they choose to play it safe and disengage themselves from the education process. They are refusing to participate in class, do their homework, or study for tests. They act out in the classroom, join gangs, and drop out of school.

Not all of the pressure to "dumb down" is from peers. Sometimes it is from their families and other adults who think it's just fine to do without an education. Some parents think that having an education, just like speaking correctly, is selling out or "acting White." They fail to understand that a parent's role is to help his child have a better, safer, and more prosperous life. A parent's duty is to recognize, seek out, and provide his child with opportunities to excel and grow into the best person he can be. This process helps both the family's standard of living and the community's well-being. It is just shortsighted to believe that getting an education is somehow traitorous to the Black community. If our children make only the same level of contributions to the family or community as we have made, then nothing will ever grow or progress.

It is not about "acting White" when we encourage our student to speak standard English so she will be a competitor in the job market. It is not about "acting White" for us, as parents, to have high expectations for our student, demanding that she exercise her God-given intelligence by making good grades in school. It's not about "acting White" wanting to see your student take advantage of opportunities to travel, meet different people, and learn about other cultures so he can compete in business and industry or just be able to intelligently communicate with other people.

Our hard-earned money, in the form of tax dollars, goes into the public schools in this country. Expecting and demanding that our children stay in school and get the education we are paying is our heritage too. Honor it.

# Achieving a Goal

Just as students have trouble imagining the past, they often have trouble imagining the future too. They think things happen instantaneously, and that college is so far away that planning for it is meaningless. That's one big reason why I teach goal-setting skills in my student classes as well as in my adult workshops. We all need a little training to be able to get from where we are to where we want to be.

There are four steps to successful goal achievement. A goal must be

- realistic: possible to accomplish within a reasonable amount of time.

- manageable: can be broken down into a series of steps.

- measurable: so you can tell whether you have achieved it.

- meaningful: to you, something you really want to do, rather than something you feel you *should* do.

I practice with my students, showing them that short-term goals—like passing a midterm exam—are steps toward long-term goals—like getting into college. By incorporating goals into your student's daily planner and rewarding those short-term completions, a big goal like college can become more manageable and therefore more real.

## Cultivate Your Student's Interests

Middle school is an important time to recognize your student's talents, likes, and dislikes, and nurture his abilities. There is still time to experiment with different classes in middle school, time he might not have in high school. Help him choose extracurricular activities that will benefit higher-education interests, and expose him to cultural events and activities. Know your school's policies, expectations, promotion requirements, and grade requirements for graduation. Middle school is a big jump from elementary school, but it is only a warm-up to the level of work and involvement needed in high school.

And, as always, talk about college. Don't wait. Start a savings plan with your child's input, no matter how small it seems at the outset. Let your student know that you expect them to work hard, do their best, and attend college. It's never too early to instill hopes, dreams, goals, and expectations in your children. At this age, they need to be brought on board with the goals you're aiming for. It's not enough, as it was when they were younger, to tell them, "You're going to go to college." Now the message is expanded to mean, "You're going to go to college, and these are the steps we're going to take to get you there." And that means getting tough with all the messages your student is getting from television, popular media, and peers. Remember when I talked about not being a best friend and being a positive role model? Now is the time to review those chapters and not just encourage your student to work hard but to insist on it. If you expect your student to be a smart, successful, well-spoken adult, you have to model those

117

qualities yourself. And since teens and preteens are notorious for not wanting to be seen with their parents, you can promote friendships with peers and other adults who model those traits as well.

## Manage Your Time Wisely

Opportunities to learn keep coming whether we're ready for them or not. It can seem overwhelming. Time-management skills are needed if your student is going to be able to take advantage of the extra-credit assignments and extracurricular activities that school offers on top of homework, the ones that help make a student attractive to a college admissions committee.

In my workshops, I hand every student a day-planner notebook with a calendar and all kinds of helpful information, from tables for figuring percentages to the date of the next solar eclipse. Some of these kids have never seen an appointment book or a scheduler, so we start from the very basics.

Organization is key. When they have an assignment, they put it on the calendar, then go back and put in reminders of the assignment leading up to the date. They do the same for test dates and then go back and put in reminders to study for the test on the days leading up to the test date. Encourage them to write down all important events, even the ones they don't think they will forget (like church on Sunday and school on Monday). The point is to get them in the habit of checking their day planner in the morning so they know what's coming up that day and the next. Once they can keep track of the big events, we work on managing homework time and playtime effectively so that everything gets done, every time.

As adults, many of us take these businesslike plans for granted. We often have to be able to do this kind of time management in our jobs or we won't be able to keep them. By teaching our kids to do this in school, we are giving them a true life skill that they will use for their entire lives. Chris confessed to me after his first semester in law school that his time-management skills saved his butt. Without the ability to prioritize his tasks and keep track of tests and deadlines, he said he would have flunked out in no time.

## Test-Taking 101

Your student will be taking tests almost from the minute he enters school, such as state standardized tests that measure his progress through school and his ability to remember what he has been taught. In middle school, testing begins to take on a bigger importance. Not only are the standardized tests more difficult, but the class tests become more frequent and start counting more toward your student's final grade. Test-taking skills are a must.

Parents can do a great deal toward test-taking success. The first and possibly the largest is simply knowing that a test is coming and helping your student make a plan for studying. Cramming, the practice of staying up all night right before a test and trying to jam every test fact into your head, doesn't work. True studying takes time. So find out what the test will cover, make a schedule for what to study, and then help your student stick to it. If studying with friends helps, then let your student study with friends. Some students work well in groups, some turn any group into a party. You know your student, and you know whether to allow study groups.

Before any test, there's always going to be some stress. Did I study enough? Did I remember everything? What if I don't do well? A little stress is a positive thing, since it can motivate your student to want to do well. Too much stress, and your student will be unable to hold a pencil, much less be able to take a test, so relaxation techniques are in order. Remind your student to breathe deeply, to lower his shoulders, and to remind himself that he is well prepared for the test and that the aim is to do well, not to perform perfectly. All of these test-taking strategies will come in handy when the really big tests—the college entrance exams—come up in high school.

## Emotional Health

Stress, not just test-taking stress, is a bigger concern in middle school than it was in elementary school. The hormones associated with puberty—for boys as well as girls—cause all kinds of changes, both physical and emotional, and those changes produce a lot of stress. How to act and how to fit in become huge issues. As a parent, you need to be willing and available to talk, even when it seems like your student has completely stopped communicating. Keeping all those feelings inside can lead to symptoms of depression.

The statistics on teen depression are scary. Even scarier is the number of cases that go undiagnosed and untreated. Between

3 and 5 percent of teens are clinically depressed, with twice as many girls as boys suffering from the disease. That's two million teenagers in the United States. Of those, only about a third get help. The rest struggle through it, and some don't make it. Suicide is the third leading cause of death among those aged fifteen to twenty-four (statistics courtesy of the National Institute of Mental Health).

My own daughter went through what I recognize now was depression when she was a young teen, and I'm sorry to say I missed most of the signals. Life happens so fast and furious that most of the time it is difficult to pay attention to the things that are happening around you. My marriage broke up, I moved my kids and myself halfway across the country, and we all began a new life. To say that I was busy doesn't even begin to cover it. I think that no matter how good a parent we are or we want to be, we still make mistakes. And one of my mistakes was with Corey, following our move to California.

The laughing little girl who was so athletic in elementary school—before we moved to California—suddenly became a couch potato when we hit Sacramento. She refused to try out for sports, even soccer and basketball, both of which she was very good at playing before the move. She didn't take an interest in much of anything. She attended school, but I had to push her to participate in extracurricular activities. And she had only two close friends. I knew deep in my heart that she was hurting, but I had too many other things to take care of. I didn't have time to nurse children whose father had abandoned all of our family dreams. I didn't have time to console children whose hearts were breaking for a father they loved, in spite of his negative choices. I didn't have time to have hope for reuniting our family with a mate who promised to get his act together. I didn't have time to think. I only had time to act.

Corey had always been a bit introverted and shy, but her new level of shyness was preventing her from doing much of anything. She turned more and more inward and was fast becoming a recluse. I couldn't understand what was happening to her. I figured she was just shy and not anxious to fit in. I didn't recognize that she was depressed and needless to say, I failed to get her treatment. She stayed down and out for a couple of years, but we were lucky. Once she started high school, she began coming out of her shell, and by the time she was in tenth grade, though she was still shy and introverted, she was no longer exhibiting signs of real depression. I feel very fortunate that she weathered those years without spiraling down into the negative behaviors many depressed teens adopt: an eating disorder, self-mutilation, or drugs.

As parents we are so bogged down with the basic responsibilities of keeping a roof over our kids' heads and food on the table, providing adequate physical health care, making sure they do well in school, and protecting them from harm, it's easy to forget about their mental health. We are so caught up in our own messes, we forget how those messes also affect our children. Kids feel stress and kids get depressed. Big life changes—and getting a divorce and moving across the country certainly qualify as big life changes—can trigger depression. When we separate from a partner, our kids experience the separation as well, and often in different ways. Our experiences are not limited to just us, they are far-reaching and residual.

If I had known then what I know today, I would have provided counseling or treatment for both Chris and Corey. I would have also gotten treatment for myself, to help me get through the feelings of failure, injustice, grief, guilt, and hatred I experienced. For a long time I was in denial, believing that my husband would wake up one bright morning and once again become the man I had married. And I wanted him to be that southern boy again, the one with the good manners and respect for women, the one I fell in love with. I was waiting for him to grow up and realize the gem of a family he had and the blessings God had given us. It never happened.

His betrayal hit me hard. I had promised myself I would have children only if I had someone to help me raise them. Now I was failing that promise. I was afraid of the hard times I knew were ahead, looking for a job, finding a decent community to raise my kids with good neighbors and safe schools, and being able to provide the same quality of life in California that my kids were accustomed to having in Missouri. I was afraid of failing my children, as it was now my single responsibility to insure they survive this life. I was alone and it was terrifying.

But as terrifying as it was for me, it must have been worse for Corey. Taken from the only home she had ever known and separated from her adored father, she had a dark road to travel before she could see that our life in Sacramento was a good life and that despite his actions toward his family, her father still loved her.

I am a very involved parent, and if I can miss the symptoms of depression, so can you. According to a Brown University study from 2002, even parents who enjoy a good relationship with their child, one where the lines of communication are open, don't recognize depression in their own kids, and in fact don't know what depression in teens looks like.

I'm done beating myself up about it—from all the reading I've done, even though as parents we blame ourselves for our child's mental state, we are not ultimately to blame. All we can do is recognize it for what it is and try to help. Depression has a wide range of symptoms, but no one of these by itself means your child is depressed. Here's a list for you to keep in mind:

- has trouble concentrating or making a decision

- is angry, restless, and irritable

- exhibits a drop in academic performance

- has trouble getting along with peers and siblings

- complains of headaches or muscle aches

- has low energy

- shows a sudden change in appetite or weight

- complains of insomnia

- stops caring about appearance and hygiene

- spends much more time alone

- skips classes or, if he or she shows up for class, fails to pay attention

- drops out of usual activities (sports, music, hobbies)

- has trouble expressing his or her feelings

Any parent will agree that adolescents typically display any or all of these in a given week! That doesn't mean your child is depressed. The key to whether your child may have a real problem is if the symptoms persist. If your child changes his or her behavior and mood and stays that way for two weeks or more, you need to seek professional help. Keep in mind, too, that unusually stressful periods can trigger depression. So if your teen is dealing with the death of a friend or loved one, a chronic illness, or some other trauma, be on the alert for the signs on that list. Make yourself available to listen, listen, listen.

Depression as a teen can set up a pattern that recurs when the teen is an adult, setting your child up for a long-term battle against major depression. Untreated, it can also lead to more immediate problems, like drinking and drugs, as your teenager attempts to self-medicate. Best to try to stay on top of it and get treatment when the problem starts. And don't get all caught up worrying that your child will be singled out and ridiculed for seeking psychological help. If you treat this as a medical issue and the need to see a specialist as merely "going to the doctor," you can deflect that kind of peer misbehavior. And besides, the important thing is to get help if you feel it's needed.

We were lucky that we all survived this period in our lives. Corey has gone on to lead a full and healthy life. She has even forgiven her father, something I still struggle with, and I can now look back at all the upheaval in our lives and realize that the three of us were all working hard to keep everything together and focus on our goals.

I'm a big believer in pushing hard. The world is a difficult place, and if our children are going to succeed in it, they have to know how to work. Your student may not be the next Nobel Prize–winning scientist, but she is certainly never going to get anywhere if she isn't focused on a goal. Not all students are going to be academically brilliant, but all students *can* achieve. Sometimes in middle school, because of the increased peer pressure and the effect of the hormones running through their bodies, students will start to fall away from the college-bound path. It is up to the parents to remind them—to push them if necessary—back on track.

## Miss Sharon Says

**Grow Your Student's Interests:** Bring home books, games, and toys related to the subjects your student likes. Encourage exploration by visiting museums, galleries, factories, parks, and businesses.

**Emphasize Education as a Right:** Find creative ways to encourage the kind of thinking you want from your student. Even something as simple as a wall calendar in your kitchen featuring twelve people famous for their contributions to science, history, or the arts shows your commitment to valuing education.

**Take Puberty in Stride:** If you need help talking to your student about the changes happening to his or her body, get help. There are plenty of books and Web sites on how to start and continue potentially embarrassing conversations. See the Resources section at the end of the book for suggestions.

**Recognize Depression for What It Is:** Don't overreact to every little mood swing. Keep a journal of any behaviors that seem indicative of depression and if you see a pattern over time, seek help.

# Chapter 6

# High School and Higher

# Expectations

I am an advocate for my kids, in the truest sense of the word. I made it my responsibility to inform all of their high school teachers, counselors, and principals that our family goal was for them to attend college. I would ask, "How can you help us get there, and what do we need to provide for you, and what do we need to do to help ourselves?" Understand that teachers who have any love for their profession want to be a part of their students' successes. When you, the parent, inform a teacher that the family has high expectations for their student, then that teacher takes on a whole different attitude with the student. The teacher begins to nurture, encourage, challenge, and motivate that student toward success.

But the teacher is only one part of the equation. The student and the parent have to stay just as motivated. When Chris started high school, I started my habit of keeping track of his absences and tardies on my calendar at home. If he was absent from school, I made a note. If he missed the opening bell because of a dentist appointment, I made a note. When his report card came home, I checked the number of days he was reported out or tardy, and I verified it against my records. The days tallied, and I knew Chris wasn't skipping school or showing up late without a good reason. This was a pretty easy way to keep tabs on him, and he knew I was doing it and I don't think it bothered him. In a way, it pleased him that I cared so much.

One semester in his junior year, he came home with a report card that showed three times as many days absent from school as I had on my calendar. When I asked him about it, he looked at the report card and his eyes got very wide.

"That must be a mistake, Mom," he said. "Maybe there was an error in the computer." He assured me that he had not been skipping school.

While I was prepared to believe him, I also needed to check with the school to make sure. The next morning, I went with Chris before school to the vice principal's office and showed him the report card with the excessive number of absences. He spoke up immediately.

"Oh, Ms. Chandler, I'm so sorry. We are planning to notify all the parents that there was a glitch in the reporting of the days absent for all the kids. I don't think any of them went out correct. Chris was here when he says he was here."

I was relieved that everything was all right, and as I left his office the vice principal said to me, "Hundreds of report cards went out with the wrong number of absences, but you're the only parent who has called or stopped in to check up on it."

I reminded him that I have the highest expectations for my children and that they are supposed to attend class every day.

Chris smiled and said, "Yeah, my mom's on it. We don't even try stuff because we know we can't put anything over on her."

I had to laugh at how well my son understood me!

I also had to inform the vice principal that I would be in his office anytime something came up during Chris's four years at that school, because my children and I were college bound. Anything that threatened to derail that goal needed my immediate attention. One of my first high school visits, even before that day in the vice principal's office, was to the counselor's offices.

## Good Counseling Counts

I stress this in every workshop and class I teach: You have to get to know the school's counselors. Make sure they know what your expectations are for your student, and enlist their help in keeping your student on a college path. You and your student should become your high school counselor's best friends. Make appointments, and I mean several, throughout the four years, to discuss all of the possibilities and then visit, together, the college resource center. You should learn how to do the research along with your student, and book time to surf the Internet, look at catalogs, and sample applications.

You have to keep track of what your student needs to graduate from high school. It's great to be college bound, but you have to achieve high school first. State requirements vary, and even within states requirements change, so talk to your student's school for the current graduation minimums. Here is your checklist of all the basic things you need to keep in mind in high school. Don't be afraid to add things to my list—this is just a starting place for you.

- Meet with teachers and counselors every year.

- Discuss your higher-education goals with teachers and administrators every year, and in between as needed.

- Encourage the teachers at your school to contact you to voice any concerns they have about how your student is performing in their class or in school in general.

- Know the course requirements your student needs to graduate and refer to them often.

Growing up in the Midwest during the sixties and seventies, I attended a segregated elementary school and later an integrated middle and high school. In elementary school, as you have previously read, my intellect and spirit were nurtured by my African American teachers. I knew I was intelligent and special. I had very high aspirations for myself. When I left elementary school and began seventh grade at an integrated middle school, since my grades had been excellent, I was placed in the accelerated program. But at my new school, I struggled to keep up. My elementary education, it turned out, was considered academically inferior, and to some degree it was true. I was ill prepared for the level I would be expected to rise to in middle school. I don't blame my school. I blame the system.

I can tell you firsthand how White schools in the 1960s sent us their used and outdated textbooks just before they were ready to put them in the trash. We would spend whole class periods erasing the answers from used workbook pages or taping torn pages for our use the following school year. We were the victims of low expectations.

In seventh grade, I was eventually placed with the "average" kids. At least I wasn't sent with the "special" kids, who were segregated from the "normal" kids in a school of their own. The humiliation of being thought "average" inflicted wounds on my self-esteem that I can still feel today. I hated school and everything that accompanied it. Not one of my White teachers had a kind word for me. No one at this school thought I had any worth at all, and pretty soon I agreed.

Once in high school I honestly tried to be interested in my classes and extracurricular activities. I tried out for the various clubs and after-school activities like the Pen and Ink club, but my membership was never accepted, even though I took art classes all four years. I had recovered some of my natural spunk and was determined to get what I could out of my mandatory education. Then I had the required visit with my counselor. That was the nail in the coffin of my higher education career.

Just as your high school counselor can be your best resource on your road to college, in my day he could also be a major roadblock. Mr. Moran worked in a big corner office along with several other school administrators. I can close my eyes and see all of the students lined up in the hall outside his office to talk to him about their futures. Most of the students in the high school were White, so Black students were only a dot here and there, in the line of potential doctors, lawyers, teachers, or other professionals. I felt inspired by all that talent, lined up and waiting to be sent off into the world.

Mr. Moran was not much taller than I was, but his size was no reflection of his power over me. He was still a White man, and therefore an authority. Most of my experiences involving him came at the closing of the school year, when counselors helped students choose classes for the coming semester. At the conclusion of my junior year, I expected him to discuss with me the classes I needed to complete to be eligible to apply for college the following year, but the only so-called help I received was advice on how I must further my secretarial training. He never opened any of the hundreds of college brochures that lined the bookcases and shelves of his office. He never asked me what I wanted, or took the trouble to find out which classes interested me, or in which I excelled. In the Gospel According to Mr. Moran, girls like me only needed to take typing and shorthand classes so we could then get secretarial jobs after high school. He refused to talk with me about college. He refused to help me figure out which subjects I needed to take to become eligible for any education beyond high school, and certainly not college. He refused to discuss my talents or my dreams for my life as an adult. I had no one to advocate for me, since my mother had not been invited to any meetings. I felt intimidated by his office and his position—if not by Mr. Moran himself—and assumed he knew best.

I had imagined myself as an artist, a writer, a lawyer, or an architect. When he told me that all I could ever hope to be was someone's secretary, I literally gave up. I didn't care about making passing grades or excelling in any subject. I turned my attention to demonstrations and fighting for causes seldom my own.

In the two years I took typing and shorthand, I remember passing only one timed test. I loved art, band (I played the clarinet), and English literature classes. I begged Mr. Moran to enroll me in the woodwork class that only boys were allowed to take. I don't need to tell you that he said no. I have always been intrigued by the history of buildings and by their development, planning, and construction. I yearned to create, and to learn the principles behind the creations of others I admired. But that dream went nowhere, because the person who should have been encouraging my dream was steadily and relentlessly killing it.

I have often since thought of the number of dreams this counselor may have squashed. He had so much power. He could have nurtured the next astronaut or civil rights leader, or a future world-renowned artist or symphony maestro. Who knows how many dreams he disintegrated with his keep-you-in-your-place attitude?

*You can't rely on your school counselor to nurture your student's dreams.* You, too, have to do everything in your power to expand your student's horizons.

You need to show your student how to take advantage of all the opportunities that become available in these high school years. That means that you have to be on top of what's going on at school. Just because your student does not bring home the flyer about the math club that's forming doesn't mean you shouldn't sign him up. You have to have your own channel of information from the school to you that does not rely on your student to deliver paperwork.

Every parent needs to become a stage mom, pushing them to try new things, encouraging them to step outside of their comfort zones, and making them finish any project they might start. It helps if you tie activities into things you know your student is already interested in. Just like encouraging your student to read by bringing home books that deal with favorite subjects, science, math, and social studies can be related to popular culture. Skateboarding can be a way to study physics. Budgeting and shopping for clothes is a great lesson in economics. Using their interests keeps students engaged.

My kids always went to summer school and attended zero period during the school year. It didn't matter that they didn't need to take extra classes—they used zero period (the hour before the school day begins) to have club meetings, to do homework, or to make final preparations for class. I made it clear that when I left for work in the morning, the kids left the house too.

When Chris was in tenth grade, he was in a study group within one of his English classes. One Sunday afternoon, I received a call from his teacher, informing me that Chris's group included several boys who were the class cutups, and that the group as a whole was not taking their assignments seriously. Out of concern for Chris's grade, she asked me to intervene by suggesting to Chris that he choose another study group. I agreed to talk with Chris and when I did, we agreed that he would make the move the following day. I was surprised, therefore, to receive yet another phone call from his teacher on the following Sunday. She repeated her concern for Chris's grade, since Chris had made no move to get out of that study group. Thinking that my talk with Chris had solved the problem, I hadn't even thought to follow up with the teacher, and here it was a week later and nothing had been done. I assured her that the situation would be resolved, once and for all.

The following day, I appeared at the classroom door and asked the teacher if I could bring Chris outside for a little private discussion. I proceeded to read him the riot act, letting him know how disappointed I was that he had failed to obey my instructions. He had lied to me when he said he would

"Why do I have to go to college?"

You are sure to hear this from your student at least once. Have your answers ready in terms they can understand.

- A college education will get you a better job and then help you keep it.

- College graduates earn more money—even a two-year degree makes a difference in income.

- College gives you a good start in life (general knowledge makes you a more interesting person!).

| EXAMPLES OF JOBS YOU CAN GET WITH A TWO-YEAR DEGREE | EXAMPLES OF JOBS YOU CAN GET WITH A FOUR-YEAR DEGREE | EXAMPLES OF JOBS YOU CAN GET WITH A POSTGRADUATE DEGREE |
|---|---|---|
| Computer Technician | Computer Systems Analyst | Scientist |
| Registered Nurse | Pharmacist | Doctor |
| Commercial Artist | Graphic Designer | Architect |
| Auto Mechanic | FBI Agent | Lawyer |
| Surveyor | Engineer | Zoologist |

Source: Information from U.S. Department of Education.

Geometry and algebra are key. According to statistics from the U.S. Department of Education, 71 percent of low-income students who took geometry in middle school went to college. Getting a solid grounding in math frees you up to take physics, trigonometry, and other Advanced Placement courses in high school.

Make sure your student is taking *and working hard to pass* math, English, science, and history. Consider taking computer science classes, and don't neglect the arts. Middle school is the perfect opportunity to plan for the next six years and beyond, since you now have a choice of classes.

make the move, and I do not tolerate a liar. I reminded him of our family goal—his attending college and the importance of each grade and class toward that goal. I also informed him that this would be the last time we would discuss his reassignment to another group, and that I would not be visiting his class again under the same circumstances. I made sure I made my points loud enough so that his classmates and teacher could overhear. I guarantee you, inside that classroom you could've heard a pin drop. I had everyone's attention. That was the last time I had to show up at school like that. His teacher thanked me for my visit. By the end of the semester, Chris received a hard-earned A in that class.

I knew that my insistence that he leave that study group was a hard move for him to make. He did not want to appear as the smart kid and alienate himself from the group by making them feel inferior or rejected. He had to save face with his peers so he lied to me. I eventually understood that I needed to be the bad guy in this situation and not let peer pressure rule over Chris's welfare. Because I made my case so loudly, he could make it clear to his friends that he was forced to move and that he wasn't putting them down in any way.

Peer pressure plays a big role in the life of a high school student, and nowhere is this more evident than in the pressure to experiment with alcohol, tobacco, and drugs. Addressing the problems of alcohol and drugs is one that plagues almost every family in America. Every family knows someone who smokes, who is doing drugs, has a drug-related legal violation (driving while intoxicated), or is in rehab.

Keeping our children away from alcohol, tobacco, and drugs is impossible. Kids experiment to find out what the feeling of intoxication is all about. My goal with Chris and Corey was to raise children who would be strong enough to try drugs just once, or strong enough to "just say no."

Moving Chris and Corey out of my husband's house while they were teens was probably one of the best and most important decisions I ever made. I could now totally control the use of alcohol, drugs, and tobacco by the adults in my home. I did not smoke or do drugs and only occasionally drank a glass of wine. My impressionable teens would not receive mixed messages from me concerning those vices. Whether they experimented with drugs without my knowing, I don't know. It's possible, but Chris was always an athlete, taking care of his body with good nutrition and exercise, and Corey was such a homebody that I honestly didn't worry about it. I think that by staying close to both kids, knowing their friends and being involved in their activities, I let them know that I wanted only the best for them. They knew I would be disappointed if they showed by giving in to peer pressure that they could not make positive decisions for themselves.

## High School, Year by Year

For the parents in my Transitioning to Middle School workshop, I always run through the four-year expectations for high school students. The parents are usually a bit overwhelmed by the idea of high school, but with plenty of information and early training, by the time their student attends high school the parents are prepared and know what to expect.

When a student becomes a *freshman*, everything starts to count toward graduation and college. Freshman courses, grades,

## Statistics on Drug Use

Number of adult smokers of tobacco who started smoking in high school: 80%
(1994 U.S. Surgeon General's Report)

Number of high school seniors and dropouts who reported either getting drunk, binge drinking, or drinking and driving: 80%

Number who said that drinking had caused them to feel sick, miss school or work, get arrested, or have a car crash: more than 50%
(Ellickson, P. L., et al. "Teenagers and Alcohol Misuse in the United States: By Any Definition, It's a Big Problem." *Addiction* 91(10):1489–1503, 1996)

Number of eighth graders who have consumed alcohol: 52%

Number of eighth graders who have smoked cigarettes: 41%

Number of eighth graders who have used marijuana: 20%
(Substance Abuse: The Nation's Number One Health Problem at http://www.gdcada.org/statistics/teens.htm)

and credits all become part of a student's transcript, and freshman grades are used in determining a student's grade point average (GPA). Freshman activities, honors, and awards can also be listed on college and scholarship applications. High school is the big time! All that preparation you've been doing, developing good habits and encouraging academic excellence, will really start to show in high school.

This doesn't mean you can slack off with any of the involvement you've already practiced. Your teen might not act like it, but your involvement in their school is still important to them. Now is the time to become familiar with high school graduation requirements. Sit down and figure out with your student which classes she should be taking. Investigate test requirements. If your high school has an exit exam—a test your student must pass in order to graduate—you should know about it now. Continue to attend any parent-teacher conferences, and start going to college financial aid nights and/or college fairs. No, it's not too early. While you're at it, look into any career orientation programs or resources, and visit the college resource center. Familiarize yourself with these things now—you're going to be using them a lot in the next few years.

*Sophomore* year is an important one for personal growth and the development of the interests that will carry your student into an adult future. No longer a freshman but not yet an upperclassman, the sophomore has a certain amount of freedom to explore. Use it! Get your student involved in any activities that interest her—you're working on identifying strengths, abilities, aptitudes, and interests here, so encourage a wide range of possibilities.

- Keep track of academic progress to make sure goals are being met.

- Testing starts in tenth grade, so you need to prepare for practice SATs and ACTs.

- Join career development clubs on campus.

- Volunteer!

- Keep college in the conversation.

*Junior* year is when students need to think seriously about their postsecondary options. College tests, college visits, and the search for scholarship money begin now. Aren't you glad you know where the college resource center is?

As a junior, your student needs to register to take the SAT (Scholastic Aptitude Test) and the ACT (which used to stand for American College Testing but now goes only by the acronym ACT). If test-taking isn't your student's strong suit, then you might want to consider taking a course specially designed to help kids get through the SAT. Ask at your counselor's office or look online for a course near you. While you're online, you can investigate colleges. Send away for brochures from any that meet your requirements (you'll need to read the college chapter in this book first). Take the time to narrow the choices down to about six, seven, or eight colleges that your student could see himself attending. And, as always, keep an eye on general academic progress. Slips in grades now can still be remedied in summer school.

Everything comes together for a *senior*. The rewards of all the hard work become visible. You still need to keep careful track of dates of tests, college application deadlines, and scholarship application deadlines. Academics can't be allowed to fall victim to senioritis (the disease that affects those soon to be graduated): Despite senior parties, senior proms, and senior status, homework still has to be done and projects still need to be completed. Once applications are done and college acceptances start arriving in the mail, you need to help choose a college.

It's easy to get overwhelmed by the demands of high school. Your student could easily feel lost or drowning. If they didn't get time-management lessons in middle school, now is the time for a crash course.

In their four years of high school, they need to learn such things as how to take notes, how to do research, and how to

## Taking the SAT

The Scholastic Aptitude Test (SAT) is a standardized test that colleges use as one measure of a student's scholastic achievement. Every college applicant has to take it! Admissions committees at colleges across the country need some kind of yardstick to measure a student from a small private high school in Denver against a student from a big public school in Pittsburgh. They both take the same test.

The good test-taking skills learned in school can help here. Remember the basics:

Study early, and take it slowly. Don't try to cram.

Practice. The PSAT (Preliminary SAT) is designed to give students a low-stakes chance to take the SAT and find out where they need to work harder and where they are already up to speed. It also introduces the format of the test so it isn't a surprise on SAT day.

Be healthy. A good night's sleep, a healthy breakfast, and moderate exercise between bouts of studying can make a big difference.

write up the results of both. Good study habits learned earlier need to be reinforced. Students also need to keep up with the technology around them. Kids usually don't have a problem with this, but as parents we have to remember to encourage what we ourselves might not be all that tuned into. Computers and the Internet are necessary to a student's survival, so typing classes are a must.

At the same time, a college-bound student needs to take as much math and science as is offered as well as all their college-required courses. If you think this sounds easy, then try running it by your teenager. They'll tell you it can be fiendishly difficult. But it's not impossible.

The U.S. Department of Education recommends the following for high school students:

Four years of **English**. That includes literature (American and other) and writing.

Three to four years of **mathematics**. We're talking geometry, algebra I and II, trigonometry, and calculus.

Two to three years of **history** and **geography**. U.S. history and government are required, but world history and cultures, geography, and civics are also needed.

Two to three years of **science**. Biology, chemistry, physics, and earth sciences.

At least one year of **visual and performing arts**. Including art, drama, dance, and music.

One to three years of *challenging* **electives**. No, study hall does not count as a challenging elective. Try computer science, communications, economics, or statistics.

Two to three years of a **foreign language**. Many colleges require that a student pass a proficiency exam, so *habla Español* or *sprechen Deutsch,* just get your student to a language lab. Note: All of the years must be of the *same* language, not two years of Spanish and one of German.

As if this weren't enough, colleges are looking for students with a solid grounding in nonacademic subjects as well. Participation in service clubs, church, sports, or any volunteer activity is, to a college admissions officer, an indication of a well-rounded person and an attractive candidate for college admission. Even better, if your student takes a lead role in student government, school spirit groups, or extracurricular activities, then colleges are going to notice and respond favorably.

## Help Is Available

Parents can always use a little outside help raising their children. For me, this is one of the most important aspects of my workshops. The parents who come to me need my help, and I feel privileged to be able to provide it. We all need help; it takes a strong person to ask for it. We need help from babysitters, housekeepers, repairmen, and other professionals to keep our children and households safe and running efficiently. Why not get help from people who have a genuine interest and investment in our children? I like to think of these mentors as an extension of the family, as "villagers" who are available to give kids experiences and opportunities they would never receive under normal circumstances. Both of my kids have had mentors throughout their lives.

Chris's mentors have included men I trusted and knew were genuinely good, God-fearing people with whom I was proud to associate. Men like my former boss, Peter Solomon, who showed Chris how to dig ditches properly in his backyard and install professional-quality plumbing. There was also Lawrence Holland and his wife, who gave Chris an after-school job traveling and working on a sno-Kone truck at festivals throughout northern California. Lawrence later hired Corey and her friend Cassie for the same position. Following a very long and tiring weekend of digging out ice for the sweet treats, Corey told me, "There's no question in my mind that I am getting a college education, because I know that I was not made to do manual labor." Chris adopted as role models, at one time or another, the fathers of his friends, my coworkers, and even a few of the men I've dated. I always made it a point to introduce my kids to people I felt good about and who had proven they could be trusted.

Corey's mentor, her high school teacher Mrs. Herndon, nurtured and encouraged her to run for president of the Math Engineering Science Achievement (MESA) program at Florin High School. Corey developed interpersonal skills and blossomed as a leader under her tutelage. For one semester she also participated in another program where a female police detective mentored her. This innovative program involved Corey in her first snow skiing experience in the mountains of Nevada, and included sleepovers with other girls at Corey's school.

When Corey first told me of wanting to participate in the mentoring program, I had mixed emotions about the prospect of some other woman teaching my daughter. I felt that I should be the one to take my daughter on those special outings and enjoy the experience with her. I also felt that if I wasn't so financially strapped all of the time, I would be able to afford to do special things with my kids. As I look back on my feelings now, I realize that half of my hesitation was out of jealousy and the other half stemmed from guilt. I'm glad now that I didn't let my own selfish feelings interfere with Corey's opportunities to learn new things and meet and develop relationships with very interesting people. Part of being a good parent is allowing other people to teach your children.

You can also consider yourself a mentor of the teens around you. It can be mutually rewarding to keep in touch with your kids and their friends. It is so easy to pull back when your kids seem to need to you less, but I'm telling you, you have to stay connected to their lives. To do that, you have to spend time with them. Make your house the group hangout, and be the kind of person they don't mind having around. If that doesn't sound like something you want to do, think again. Wouldn't you rather have them at your house than on the street corner?

With just a few simple steps, you can create a safe haven for teens. First, make it clear that you welcome your teenager's friends by extending them the respect and kindness you would show any guest. Talk to them not as children but as fellow adults. And while you don't want to become the Junk Food Hangout, if you keep real food in the house and available to your guests, you will endear yourself to teens.

Then, take them where they want to go. Many kids can't drive, and even if they can, they don't necessarily have a car. A willingness to be the Taxi Mom goes a long way toward establishing friendly ties. When Chris and Corey were teens, we would load up the minivan with eight, nine, ten kids and sneak into the drive-in. Corey and I would sit in the front seat and everyone else would be in the dark back of the van covered with blankets. So we only paid for two people to get in, and everyone else got to pocket their five dollars and buy refreshments instead. We would choose a spot and you'd see eight kids leap out with lawn chairs and we'd all watch the movie.

In the course of picking up these kids and driving to and from the movie, though, I heard more about who liked whom, who was in trouble, and who was unhappy. They talked in front of me because they knew I could be trusted not to laugh at them or trivialize their problems. They would ask me questions about sex and I would tell them the truth. I also entertained them with stories about my own life—which they found funny and bizarre—so they felt they knew me and could talk to me. I heard their confidences and even got asked for advice about how to handle their romantic relationships. Their friendship at that age was worth more to me than being a good citizen and paying for a carload of kids at the drive-in.

I recently ran into a friend of Chris's while I was having lunch with a girlfriend. He came up to our table and said, "Are you Ms. Chandler?" I didn't recognize this huge man, but when he said, "I'm Don," I remembered him as one of Chris's good buddies from high school. He sat with us for a few minutes and I filled him in on what was happening in our lives, and then he turned to my girlfriend and said, "You know what she used to do? She used to put us all in the back of her van and sneak us into the drive-in. Man, that was great. We had so much fun." I had to laugh that he remembered that, but I was also reminded that as much as *I* had enjoyed those outings, I had been making lasting memories for those kids as well.

## Do It All

High school offers so many opportunities for kids; I tell my workshop parents to take advantage of them all, but in real life no one can. Take on as many as you can, then, and work with your student to decide which programs—curricular or extracurricular—make the most sense for her. Programs like special interest clubs, music, choir, theater, sports, cheer, dance, and academic competition are just some of the programs available to students in high school. And that's just through school. All those things exist outside of school, plus there are activities like Scouting, community volunteering clubs, church groups, and social clubs that can be related to school or completely separate. These activities are not only a good way to show on a college application that a student is well rounded, they can provide academic and personal advancement, not to mention maturity and self-esteem.

Advanced Placement (AP) classes are college-level courses offered in high school. While AP classes offer a deeper look into the subject they cover and therefore greatly increase the student's knowledge of the subject, they have other benefits as well. At the end of the school year, students take the AP exam in the subject they're studying. If they pass, the class is then an equivalent to a semester of college. Take enough AP classes and pass enough AP exams and your student starts college with some of the basic requirements out of the way. This strategy is both a money saver (you're not paying for college credits) and a time-saver (your student's college schedule now has room for other things beyond English 101). AP classes also look good on your student's college application, since they are a good indication that he can handle college-level material.

You have a powerful role as a parent. As much as it's true that your kids are going to be the people they are meant to be no matter what you do, it is also true that your encouragement (and discouragement) will shape their path in life. Help your student make the right educational decisions that will lead to a degree and a productive career. Be involved in your student's subject choices, schools, and extracurricular activities. Dream along with them—fight the dream destroyers and don't become one yourself. It is up to you to keep a wary eye out for the people in your child's life who will try to deflate a dreamer and head them off before they do any harm.

Helping your student decide on a field of study is just an extension of what you're already doing if you've followed the guidelines in this book. Encourage exploration, nurture their talents and preferences, and enroll them in classes that stimulate their interests. Sometimes that will mean keying into a volunteer opportunity or exploring a new extracurricular group.

While in high school, both of my kids also participated in a four-year college preparatory program, Upward Bound, sponsored by the University of California, Davis (UC Davis). The program was developed to give first-generation (no one in the family has graduated from a four-year college) low-income students the opportunity to attend college. From the end of their sophomore high school year through the end of their freshman year in college, they spent six weeks of each summer vacation (summer residential program) attending the university taking individualized academic and special-interest classes, earned up to ten high school elective credits, and experienced the college environment. For six great weeks, they lived in the campus dorms, attended classes, visited the Oregon Shakespeare Festival in Ashland, Oregon, camped out for several days, participated in a talent show, and staged their own graduation festivities.

During the school year, university students tutored and counseled the Upward Bounders (UB'ers), helped plan holiday parties and get-togethers, and took the high school students on statewide college tours. That is how Chris and Corey decided on the schools they would attend. Chris first chose the University of California at Irvine but he finally decided to attend UC Davis. Most important, the Upward Bound program helps students prepare for the college entrance test (SAT). I have become a self-appointed spokesperson for the program because it works! The staff works diligently to improve each student's grade point average, increase their learning skills, helps to elevate the student's self-esteem and confidence and enrich their academic and social development. Each summer when Chris and Corey returned home, I witnessed a new maturity in them. They were more serious about their academic performances.

Upward Bound isn't the only college prep program in the world. Use your student's summers to expand and enrich their education. College campuses often sponsor internships for high school students. They also offer tours and outreach to high schoolers looking for a taste of the college experience. As parents, we have to look for the programs in our region and encourage our high school student's participation.

Look into innovative programs like UC Berkeley's California Early College Academy. This program allows disadvantaged high school students to finish high school while earning college credits, kind of like a small college inside a high school. Funded by the Gates Foundation's Early College High School Initiative, tuition is free and students are admitted based on socioeconomic need. And I wouldn't be doing my duty if I didn't point out what a great program Upward Bound is; check online to see if a university near you features a UB course. Another option to look into is school-to-work programs like the Regional Occupational Program (ROP), which offers tuition-free off-campus on-the-job training during high school hours. This helps kids develop job skills and investigate possible career choices. They even receive high school credits for school-approved jobs. ROP classes are open to anyone sixteen years and older. Students receive classroom orientation, then are placed at a training site four days a week and return to the classroom one day a week. While most jobs in the program do not offer a wage, some do, and some also offer a vocational certification process.

# So Many Choices

Helping our kids make tough decisions is a big part of parenting. It's not just about choosing college, sometimes it's about making a choice between what's wanted and what's needed. All through their lives we have to show our kids how to reason and think things out by viewing the pros and cons of any situation. Practice making sound decisions should begin early, as I've discussed above. And it doesn't end when the kids hit high school—you may think they've reached the age of reason, but your guiding hand is still needed for a shove in the proper direction.

Chris tried out for the reserve basketball team during his freshman year at Florin High School. Somewhat to my surprise, he made it. I could not remember Chris being much of a basketball enthusiast earlier in his life, but I was all for his involvement in sports as long as it didn't interfere with his studies, but the dip in his grades that inevitably corresponded with basketball season was always made up in summer school. And as you'll learn from this book, a college-bound student needs more than academics to look attractive to a college. Involvement in sports is a valuable building block in a college application.

For weeks, he faithfully attended practices and for weeks he sat on the bench, firmly established as a second-string player. He was occasionally injected into the last remaining minutes of the game when his team was well ahead. Basketball was more of a hobby, something recreational to pass the time, and a good way to belong to something big. It wasn't a bad way to attract the girls either.

He kept working at his on-court skills and finished his junior year on the varsity team. We all understood he wasn't going to win any college scholarships for his on-the-floor talents, but he was still having fun. At the beginning of his senior year, he had to try out for the varsity team, but it was understood that the tryout was just a formality. He would be on the team if he wanted it. But this year, I had a few concerns to express to him about this most important year.

Despite his best efforts, his grades always took a hit during basketball season—never enough to really make me think seriously that he should quit the team, but enough to make me concerned. The nights of practice immediately following the school day usually lasted until late in the evenings, sometime past 9:00 p.m. He would then be up doing homework well past midnight. The summer between his junior and senior years he had to attend summer school to get his GPA back up to a 3.0. This really concerned me, as this was now his final year and he would not have the summer to raise his GPA before graduation. Our agreement that basketball came second to academics seemed to have gone out the window.

Chris and I had a serious talk. We discussed the possibility that he would get an athletic scholarship as opposed to an academic scholarship, and even he agreed that the potential lay with the latter. I suggested he seriously think about our family goal of his attending college and how difficult it would be for him to maintain his current grade point average during the upcoming basketball season. He needed to decide if he wanted to play badly enough to suffer the stress and strain of playing catch-up in order to get into the college of his choice. He also needed to come to grips with the fact that he most likely was not a good enough player to play college ball. And finally, he needed to ask himself if playing basketball was important enough to him to be considered his passion.

I told Chris I would support his decision, and that I would even help by providing tutoring or other academic help if he wanted to continue to play. We left it at that. He went to the tryouts and he was chosen for the team. That day, he came to me and informed me of his decision to forego the basketball season in favor of maintaining the grade point average that would put him in the best position to choose a college. He said it was a no-brainer.

I was so proud of him. He had weighed all of the factors and made a decision that I know was difficult but that was ultimately to his advantage. When I tell this story to parents in my workshops I am often asked if I squashed Chris's dreams or dampened his spirit by being so blunt with him about his lack of talent for basketball. I believe that parents have a responsibility to be honest with children. It's one thing to support and nurture them in their dreams but it's another thing to build false hope. By encouraging him to aim high, reality and experience revealed to me and to Chris that his academic talent far outweighed his athletic abilities. Chris showed a maturity beyond his years by opting for the college education as opposed to a not-very-good chance of playing ball.

Our kids face tough decisions every day. Deciding whether to experiment with drugs, sex, or succumb to peer pressure can be life-or-death choices. It could mean life or death if the parent has not assisted him in developing reasoning skills resulting in sound, positive decisions.

# Miss Sharon Says

**Track Your Student:** You can't put an electronic monitoring device on your teen, but you can insist on staying informed. Consider funding a cell phone to make communication easier.

**Know Your School Counselors:** Don't wait until your student has a discipline problem. Start your relationship on a positive note: Stop in with cookies and a smile to introduce yourself and your student.

**Enlist the Help of Mentors:** Mentors can be found in many places outside of school and formal mentoring organizations. Look in your church, family, recreation center, and neighborhood for likely candidates.

**Research Enrichment Programs:** Check your student's backpack daily for handouts, flyers, and notes addressed to parents, especially during the first month or two of school. Much of the information related to special programs—afterschool tutoring, early college preparation, etc.—is sent home in this time frame, and you can't rely on your student to remember to deliver it to you. You have to stay on top of it.

# Chapter 7

# Choosing the Right College

You've been working hard to lay the foundation for a good college experience, and now you have to take the next big step: college itself. But which one? There are so many options, it's not surprising that you would feel a little overwhelmed. Try not to worry. As with all the previous stages you've navigated with your student, this one is manageable too.

I stress in every college-bound workshop I teach that parents and students must plan their higher education together. You must *both* do the research. Discuss with your student the pros and cons of private versus public colleges or universities. Parents and students should also take into consideration the student's learning style, personality, and maturity level. My son, Chris, has always been a very social person. He had a lot of friends, male and female, throughout high school. He played varsity basketball and had an active social life. He loves being around people and interacting with them. He chose to attend a public university with lots of social activities and a large population and campus. Learning in an environment that didn't afford him much individual attention, or having the professor recognize him, were not concerns.

My daughter, Corey, on the other hand, knew that she was shy and introverted. In middle and high school, she didn't have many close friends. She once told me, after I expressed my concern that she should make more friends (because I had quite a few friends and didn't want her to miss out on the great fun I had), that she only needed two good friends. Corey chose St. Mary's College, a private school in the San Francisco Bay Area. Because of its isolation (located deep in the canyons, only one road in and out) there would be few distractions from her studies, and the smaller classrooms would promote a one-on-one relationship with each of her professors, getting her the assistance she might need with her studies. Of course, she was right.

My ex-husband and I never let up on telling our kids that they would go to college. The college Thomas had all picked out for them was the Massachusetts Institute of Technology (MIT). I still don't know how or why he chose that school from the thousands of others, but I figured it at least gave us the moon to aim for. All of their young lives they *knew* they would someday attend MIT.

When Chris, Corey, and I arrived in Sacramento, Chris was just entering his freshman year at Florin High School. Of course I read all of the paperwork and flyers he brought home in his backpack and soon learned of a college recruitment night scheduled at a local Hewlett-Packard office. We both agreed we should go.

Entering the auditorium that night, we could see hundreds of parents and kids going from table to table filling plastic bags with all types of brochures and information on colleges. This was my first college night too; I think I was as excited as Chris! Immediately, Chris received his bag and began the process of collecting the information we could look at later that evening at home. After browsing on my own for a few minutes, I heard his voice shout, "Mom, over here, over here!"

Locating the voice, I saw his familiar face and the huge eyes and grin towering over the crowd. Chris was waving me over to the booth sporting the banner for MIT.

"Mom, he says that I *can* go to MIT! I really can go there!" The recruiter behind the desk told Chris that there were all types of opportunities in the way of internship programs, financial aid packages, and mentors who would help him if he kept his grades up and followed their plan for admission. Chris drank in that man's every word and walked away from the event with the realization that MIT was really a place he could aspire to going, and that Mom and Dad hadn't been talking out of the sides of their mouths all his life. He knew that MIT was considered one of the best schools in the nation and that he was good enough to attend that school; now the dream was believable—the recruiter had told him so. It wasn't enough to have the dream coming from his parents. He had to find out for himself, and let the dream take root.

As it turned out, MIT wouldn't have been a good fit for Chris, but we couldn't know that until we had all the information. You don't know which college suits your student until you get all the facts. UC Davis, where Chris spent his four undergraduate years, was not his first choice of colleges either. By the time he was a senior in high school, he wanted to move to Southern California and attend the University of California, Irvine. He was accepted, but I had serious concerns about throwing him to the wolves in the fast-paced SoCal world. Prior to our move to California, my kids never had to deal with gangs, people trying to sell them drugs, or any of the other big-city maladies. Even our few years in the California school system had been somewhat protected. At that time—the early 1990s—when kids in California and even on Sacramento streets were being gunned down by gang members for their Nikes and sports warm-up jackets, I still felt like I lived in a safer community than that in Southern California and that my kids were not in danger as long as they stayed close to home. Southern California was, to me, another world, and an environment I did not want my son to have to experience at such a young age.

A few months before Chris's high school graduation, a group of students attending UC Irvine were shot dead at a Los Angeles McDonald's. The only reason behind it was so the killers could steal the shoes off the students' bodies. I began reasoning with Chris that he had spent four years on the UC Davis college campus as an Upward Bound member, and it would therefore be familiar territory, one less thing to have to adjust to inside the really big adjustment to college life. He, like most teenage adventurers, wanted to get as far away from home as possible, so I also reasoned that although the Davis campus was only fifteen minutes away from Sacramento, he would be living on campus and able to lead his own life away from his family. Besides, several of his closest friends were going to Davis. He'd have a head start in that department. And

## Public or Private, College or University?

| COMMUNITY COLLEGE | STATE COLLEGE | PRIVATE COLLEGE | STATE UNIVERSITY | PRIVATE UNIVERSITY |
|---|---|---|---|---|
| offers associate's degrees | offers B.A. and B.S. degrees | offers B.A. and B.S. degrees | offers B.A. and B.S. degrees | offers B.A. and B.S. degrees |
| two-year programs | four-year programs | four-year programs | four-year programs and graduate school | four-year programs and graduate school |
| no on-campus living | may have some on-campus housing | on-campus housing available | on-campus housing available | on-campus housing available |
| low-cost classes | lower fees | higher fees | lower fees | higher fees |

there would still be plenty of new people. In short, I wanted him closer to home.

I knew I couldn't insure his ultimate safety—that would be impossible—but I knew I had to work it so that he would be living on a campus in an environment he already knew and understood. My comfort level at this point was as important as his. When my workshop parents exclaim over how I could exert so much pressure, I point out that our college goals were always a family goal, and that he and I both had to have our needs met.

# By Degrees

All degrees are not created equal. Different post–high school paths suit different students. I still believe you should aim for a four-year college, but sometimes a shorter program makes sense as a stepping-stone to a four-year university.

At one end of the postsecondary education scale is the certificate or diploma. These are granted by private career schools, by some community colleges, and as a way of marking the completion of a course of on-the-job training. These certificates can be earned in as little as a month, or they can take up to two years, depending on the institution implementing the program and the complexity of the requirements. The credits earned here may or may not be transferable to a four-year college.

An associate's degree is a two-year program offered at a community college. It is either an associate in arts (A.A.) or associate in science (A.S.) degree granted to students who complete the college's two-year program of study. On a more technical or vocational track, your student can earn an associate in applied science (A.A.S.) degree, which usually carries with it an apprenticeship requirement in their field of study.

The good news is that those two years of school can transfer over to a four-year institution when your student is ready for more. Community colleges are usually much less expensive than a four-year college, so they're an excellent way to keep the cost of a four-year education down. Be careful, though. Different schools have different rules about what kinds of transfer credit they accept. Check it out ahead of time to make sure the classes at the community college of your choice will translate into university credit. You don't want to have to pay twice for the same classes.

There are two kinds of undergraduate or bachelor's degrees: bachelor of arts (B.A.) and bachelor of science (B.S.). This is what a four-year college or university grants to a student for four (or five) years of full-time study. If you want to be able to say you have a college education, a B.S. or a B.A. is what you have to earn.

You earn a B.A. for a completed course in the humanities or liberal arts (English, social sciences, languages, and the like) and a B.S. for a completed course in the sciences (math, biology, engineering, etc.). Both require classes from a broad range of disciplines, but the majority of classes stem from the student's major field of interest.

If, after your student has earned a B.S. or a B.A., she wants to pursue a career in law, medicine, research, or business, then there's graduate school. The careers office at their university, working in close contact with your student's academic advisor, can point out appropriate programs and assist with the application process. It's just like choosing a college all over again. In graduate school, a master's degree is a one- or two-year program that extends and intensifies the education your student received in their major field of study. Corey, who majored in sociology in college, has her master's degree in sociology from Purdue University. If she wanted to take her education a step further in the same direction, she could go to school to get her doctorate (Ph.D.), which would take several additional years of study. A medical degree (M.D.) takes a further three years of study plus several more years of internship; a law degree (LL.D.) requires three challenging years of postcollege study and then a comprehensive examination (the bar exam) before a law student can become a practicing lawyer.

Before you even set foot on a college campus for a visit, you need to draw up a short list of schools that suit your student's requirements. To do this, you have to research which colleges offer what, and find out what kind of school your student is thinking of. All this can be done at college nights and in your counselor's office. Send for every brochure your counselor recommends! You can also sign up to speak to alumni of the college you're considering. Many schools have alumni groups whose job it is to talk to and recruit new students. No one can give your student a better idea of what the school is like than someone who actually attended there.

While you are looking into which colleges to apply to, you also need to make sure your student is meeting or exceeding his graduation requirements. Your counselor should provide you with a testing schedule, with pretests, dates, costs, and deadlines for registration clearly marked. Practicing filling out financial aid forms isn't a bad idea either. Teachers, counselors, administrators, and mentors who have helped your student over the years can now be asked if they will help a little further with a letter of reference. Work associates and former bosses can be asked as well. Keep a file of names, phone numbers, and all the letters you can acquire. They'll come in handy. Your student's résumé, complete with classes taken, grades achieved, a listing of extracurricular activities, and volunteer experiences should be kept up-to-date and ready for inclusion in any applications.

No matter how many times I teach my Preparing for College workshop, I always have at least one parent who comes up to me and wails, "I can't do this!" You all have to consider the alternatives. Remember the statistics I quoted. College-educated people earn better salaries, get better jobs, and in my opinion have a better shot at a good life. Putting in the time and effort now is a big investment in your student's ability to make it in this world. You don't want them sleeping on your couch forever, do you?

## Apply Yourself

There are several parts to a college application, and you can't afford to leave one out when your student applies. Entire books have been written about how to apply for college, so I'm not going to go into great detail here. The most important things to remember are what I've been telling you all along: Get organized, keep track of what's required and when, and stay on it. For nearly any college application, you'll need test scores, the written application, an essay, and recommendations. Certain schools have specific requirements, so you need to look into exactly what they want, and provide it.

College application essays are notoriously tricky to write, but they shouldn't be a reason to panic. Like any good essay, a good college essay has the following:

- A main idea that carries through the entire essay.

- Logical organization (a clear beginning, middle, and end).

- Specific evidence to support the main idea.

It also has to be accurate. This is not the place to be experimenting with big words that may or may not be used appropriately. Have another pair of eyes read it—even if your student doesn't want to hear your comments on the essay, he may be open to having a neutral third party give it a read-through. And remember not to rely on the spell-check feature in the computer to catch every error: Have your student read and reread the essay, out loud, to make sure there are no mistakes in spelling, grammar, or cohesiveness.

## Choosing a School

When you're assessing a college campus, your first task is to sort out the obvious differences between schools: size, cost, setting (urban or not), location (in-state or out), and student ratio (student to instructor as well as student gender and race). There are huge differences between Penn and Penn State, even though both are big urban schools.

Then look at the more subtle differences. When you visit colleges, sometimes you just get a feeling that the place will be right for your student. And sometimes, inevitably, you feel like something is just a little bit wrong. First, listen to what your student says to you about how she "feels" about the campus, not what she "thinks." Then examine your own feelings and try to separate the natural anxiety you may feel about your student leaving home for any genuine premonitions you may have about the campus itself. Don't try to ignore your feelings. The climate of a college campus can have a lot to do with how happy (or not) your student will be with her college experience.

What are the students like? There's a fine line between fitting in and becoming a herd animal, so you're going to need to look for a mixed population, with just enough "people like me" for your student to relate to, and a fine array of "people not like me" for her to learn to get along with.

College can be divided into two rough (and unequal) sets of factors: academic and social. You and your student have to agree on how you are going to weigh the many components of each set. Academic factors include such things as which majors are offered, which departments are particularly strong, and what will be expected from your student regarding grades, prerequirements, and mandatory classes. I would also consider the student population an important academic factor: Is this campus known as a learning environment, or are they known for their keg parties? You need to know.

On the social side, a college campus can seem overwhelming. Living situations on campus vary widely, so where to live is often a big issue. The athletic programs and activities available can influence your decision, as can the politics, religion, and gender of the place. A small women's college on the East Coast is going to exhibit a very different flavor than a large coed university in the West. I'm not saying one is better than the other. They're just different, and you have to figure out the differences and make decisions with your student.

Don't forget to look at whether the college offers a military program (ROTC), special services for the disabled (if that's a concern), and adequate campus security (especially if you're looking at schools in big cities). Even such things as when the school term begins and ends or whether it's on semesters or quarters can sway your opinion about a college.

One statistic you might not think to check up on is the number of starting freshman who actually graduate in four years. It's called the retention rate, and if it's low (like more than half of the entering students don't finish) then you need to look hard at the way that school conducts itself. (Some information from Dave Paterson's College Prep column at http://www.parent-teen.com.)

Another piece of information you'll want to consider is whether or not the school you're considering offers financial aid to its students. *U.S. News & World Report* publishes a college issue every year that lists the most generous colleges and universities in the country. The possibility of a good scholarship is another factor to feed into your decision-making process.

One thing I always tell students and their parents is that students should try to to live on campus. It's not just about getting your student out of your house, though there's that too. College life—campus life—is more than just going to class. It's about living away from home and learning how to be responsible for your own time. The bonds formed in college can last a lifetime. Unless there is absolutely no other way, college students should live at least their first year in the dorms.

## Show Them the Money

You're probably wondering by now when I was going to get around to talking about money. It's usually the first thing out of people's mouths when I talk about getting our students to college: "But I can't afford it!" I take a different approach: "You can't afford not to have them go to college." If your student works hard in school and you both do your research into the best programs for your student, then the money will come to you. It's time to utilize everything you've learned here—how to tap into your village, how to listen to your counselors—to uncover various sources of funding.

First, you have to apply. I know that sounds obvious, but you would be amazed at the number of people who tell me at my workshops that their student can't go to college because there is no money to send him, and then it turns out they didn't even fill out a financial aid application. You don't know if you qualify for aid until you get your financial aid papers back. Once that's done, then you can think about where to go. Better yet, as you're applying for colleges, have the financial aid research running right alongside the college research. That way, when he gets in (and he *will* get in somewhere if you've both done your homework), you'll have a head start on the financial aid process. Remember, many prestigious universities provide full scholarships to deserving low-income students, so don't rule out Harvard without at least looking at it. It may be just barely good enough for your student.

A parent asked me at a college prep workshop how I had managed to send both my kids to college. When I launched into my "encouraging and supporting their goals" speech, she said, "No, I mean the *money*." Oh. That.

I stress to students and parents alike, you should not always be concerned about the costs. I tell parents what I told my children: "You will be paying bills for the rest of your life, you might as well have a bill you can be proud of, the bill for your education. You need to get everything you want or need out of your education, and try to be as frugal as possible, but don't let the cost of the education keep you from getting what you think you need to be successful."

Lots of kids have paid their own way all through school. Mine did. Chris worked in campus libraries and tutoring individuals off-campus. Corey worked on campus in the Admissions Office and as a teacher's assistant. They both spent their freshman year getting accustomed to college life, but they worked every year after that. And plenty of students work their first year too. You have to discuss with your student how best to handle the first-year work situation. If you're receiving a substantial amount of aid through the work-study program, you might have to fit work into the freshman picture. If your student can't avoid working for a living as a freshman, try to find a job that doesn't involve major stress, one that can be folded into student life as easily and seamlessly as possible. For example, a front desk job in a quiet office might allow opportunities for reading and study.

I greatly impress upon my workshop participants how important it was to have each of my kids pay for his or her own education. Students appreciate their schooling more when they have worked to pay for it with their own money. Both Chris and Corey have student loans to repay, true. Loans may be hard to pay back, even with the low interest rates student loans enjoy, but it can be done, especially if a student finishes college and chooses a good career path.

Both Chris and Cory managed their education accounts as if their lives depended on keeping costs to a minimum. They took their education very, very seriously. This is *their* money they're spending, not Mom's or Dad's. Neither their dad nor I are to be sued or have our credit affected if they default on their loans. They are responsible for getting the grades, completing their studies, graduating, and paying their loans.

It would have been great if my ex-husband and I had saved up for their college education. It just didn't work out that way. What we did do is instill in them the need to get the best grades possible so that they would be eligible to receive any help that was available when they reached college age. Both have received grants, scholarships, and loans, and both have worked at work-study jobs while attending school.

At first Chris was a little slow at making scholarships and grants work for him. He didn't put in the work to research and apply, so he ended up taking out more loans than were probably necessary. He did much better in the grants department after getting the bill from the first year of his undergraduate program! The debt he was piling up was a strong motivator for him to find other sources of money. He located a needs-based scholarship for minority students as well as some money based on his intention of going to law school.

Chris's bill:

- Undergraduate at UC Davis—four years for $12,000

- Master's (one year) at USC—$30,000 (includes loans and $6,000 scholarship that paid for one class)

- Law degree (three years) at UCSD—$26,000 per year with $18,000 in scholarships per year (received loans for the remainder)

Once he got motivated, Chris did a great job finding funds and taking advantage of work-study and off-campus jobs to help supplement his income to pay for rent, food, and transportation. Although sometimes scholarships help pay some of the living expenses, seldom do they pay for all of your student's needs. Once he got to graduate school, Chris found that his departments of study often had their own scholarships to offer students. Regardless of your financial situation, if your student has good grades, makes a good case for himself at the time of application to the school, and follows through on his commitment and obligations to learning, the school will fill in the financial gaps with dollars of its own.

I like to stress to students in my classes the importance of developing a rapport with people in the financial aid department of the school. Drop by their offices so they can put a face with the name. If they like you, these people will look out for your needs by pointing you in the direction of more financial opportunities. If you are just another face to them, they will not feel the need or obligation to go the extra mile to assist you. I'm not suggesting you buy anyone in the office lunch; just be friendly, let them know who you are, and they'll take over from there.

Corey has always been a little more adventurous where the free money was concerned. She spent a lot of time her senior year of high school researching grants, talking with counselors at school, and applying to various programs for financial aid. As you can see from the figures below, she saved a big chunk of money everywhere she went. Without scholarships, her loan burden would have been nearly $200,000 by the time she finished. Corey's education bill looks like this:

- Undergraduate at St. Mary's College—$120,000. Junior and senior years she received the James Irvine Scholarship for Minority Students majoring in sociology. The scholarship also paid for her two years at Purdue working on her master's degree. Included in her tuition was one semester as an exchange student at the University of Cape Town, South Africa.

- Master's at Purdue—two years at $30,000 per year

- Master's at Loyola—two years at $20,000 per year (she's in her first year)

Corey owes the government about $70,000 so far. She has received more than $100,000 in grants and scholarships. I use my kids' actual costs in my workshops to show parents and students the difference between the total bill for a private college and the amount spent at a public university. They are always amazed at both the cost and the amount of assistance available.

Counselors do more than assist your student with class selections and college choices. They are also your first and best resource for college financial aid assistance. I like to tell the story of how, when we were first applying for financial aid, we met the first-generation-college-grad requirements for the Upward Bound program, but my household income—despite my single-mom status—was a little above the cutoff point. Chris's counselor, Ms. Stovall, suggested that I start a small business, part time, using the business deductions to reduce my gross salary so that Chris would qualify for the program. I began researching tax laws and small business requirements, learning that I could get sizeable deductions by employing my kids in the family business. I started a janitorial business, cleaning apartment complexes, houses, and businesses following construction. I worked full time for a housing program that put me in contact with general contractors who bid on large and small apartment complex renovations. We received two or three jobs per year, jobs on which I employed my kids and immediate family. By decreasing my gross income, my kids qualified for the Upward Bound program as well as for college grants, scholarships, and loans. I hadn't expected to be in a situation where I was making too much money, but with a little help from Ms. Stovall and a little research, I turned it to my family's advantage. You can too. Get the financial advice you need—whether from a high school counselor or from a finance professional—to make the best choices when applying for college financial aid.

Start researching financial aid and the many requirements for qualifying for various levels of assistance when your student is a freshman in high school. Learn what you need to know about what you can do from one year to the next so that when your student is a senior and applying for colleges, you will already have the financial picture clear in your mind. You want to be well ahead of the game and leave no room for surprises on the subject of grade point requirements or deadlines for particular forms. Paying attention to deadlines will guarantee your student the best opportunity for success.

## Savings

There are so many things we parents do for our kids. As I said before, it would have been great if I could have saved money for my kids' college educations, but I didn't. It just wasn't in the cards. They learned the value of hard work, and they know that they earned their educations in more ways than one. This doesn't mean that you can't save or that you shouldn't save for college, only that savings are one of the many ways you and

# What does College Cost?

Cost of Attendance (COA) includes:

- tuition and fees
- on-campus room and board (or a housing and food allowance for off-campus students)
- books
- supplies
- transportation
- loan fees
- dependent care and costs related to a disability (if applicable)
- miscellaneous expenses

| PRIVATE FOUR-YEAR COLLEGE AVERAGE TUITION COST PER YEAR | PUBLIC FOUR-YEAR COLLEGE AVERAGE TUITION COST PER YEAR |
| --- | --- |
| $16,332 | $3,510 |

Estimated sample budgets range from $7,024 for a student who lives at home and commutes to a two-year public college, to $24,946 for a student in on-campus housing at a four-year private institution.

(Information courtesy of College Board data at http://www.collegeboard.org/)

your student can pay for part or all of a college education. There are a wide variety of resources available to parents to save money for college even before their child is born, and just as many opportunities to start saving and continue saving throughout the child's first eighteen years.

In my workshops, I have my students calculate how much money they could save for college if they started saving, right now, one dollar a week. There are always moans and groans when I suggest this, and at least one kid will say, "We could never save enough with only a dollar a week." Take a minute to do the math. If your student is twelve years old, then there are six years left in which to save a dollar a week. Fifty-two weeks in a year, times six years. That's $312. That's a college class. Imagine saving two dollars a week. Or five. Even if you don't start when your child is born, don't let anyone tell you it's too late to start saving. It's never too late.

## Loans, Grants, and Work Study

Student loans are the number-one source of funds for college. The Federal Family Education Loan Program (FFELP), as the Guaranteed Student Loan (GSL) Program is now called, is administered by the U.S. Department of Education and state student loan guarantee agencies. In short, the federal government guarantees the loans to students funded by private lenders. Rates on these loans are often lower than for other types of loans. And yes, they have to be paid back, but the government is very patient about getting its money back, and student loans can be deferred, paid back slowly, and sometimes even partially forgiven.

When you get your financial aid papers back, it's likely that your package will consist of loans, grants, and work-study. Grants, like the federally funded Pell Grant, do not have to be repaid. Pell Grants are calculated based on need and the cost of the program in which your student is enrolled. The maximum any student can receive in one year is, as of this writing, $4,000.

Work-study is a subsidized part-time job available to your student. The biggest work-study program is through the federal government, but states and colleges may also provide money for students to earn part of their college expenses. It's a good way for your student to be intimately involved in the process of getting enough money to go to college.

I teach that college freshmen should not be expected to work during their school year, but I also know that isn't always possible. They have so many adjustments to make without having job-related stresses. They are dealing with all of the responsibilities for self, waking up in the morning without Mom's wake-up call, managing their time responsibly, trying out for the new clubs and organizations, hour upon hour of research and study, and trying to have a personal life. So if possible, try to put off that work-study job until sophomore year.

Work-study money is paid directly to the student, just like a paycheck from a real job, so you have to be careful. Since the money has been earmarked as part of the financial aid package, it should be used for housing, food, or tuition, not for the latest music or tickets to a show. Your student needs to understand this. Work-study money, since it looks an awful lot like cash, can easily slip under the budget radar and then, when there's a shortfall at the end of the year, you're going to be scrambling to make it up. Consider setting up a separate account for your student's work-study money, maybe one that takes direct deposit of that check, so the money is never actually in their hands. They would still have control of the funds in the bank, but there will be less temptation to spend the money on anything inappropriate.

## Scholarships

When my kids were applying to colleges, I actually hired someone to research the scholarships that are available for college. Today, all of that information is available for free on the Internet, at the high school college center, or at the public library.

States offer their own version of a Pell Grant to needy students. In your favorite Internet search engine (I'm a Google fan), type in the name of your state and the words *state grant* and see what pops up. Most states offer grants to students of all income levels and at every level of tuition. Again, this is free information—stay away from books and programs that ask you to pay for lists of grant programs and so-called free money. If it's free, you can find it yourself.

Scholarships are available for all kinds of reasons and to all kinds of students. If your student's high school grades are high enough along with their ACT or SAT test scores, they should be eligible for merit scholarships regardless of your financial aid status. Students should still expect to work summers or after class to meet their college costs. An after-school or weekend job, as long as it doesn't interfere with the more serious work of school, is a great way for kids to not only earn their own spending money, but it can be the beginning of their own savings account.

And a student who can demonstrate the maturity necessary to hold down a job while maintaining a decent grade point average is showing the kind of attitude needed to succeed in college.

It's important to ask the college your student is interested in attending for information on scholarships and grants that it sponsors. I know it's a lot of work to fill out form after form after form, but there's money available if you ask for it. You should apply for everything that comes your way, and you should *make* things come your way.

As I discussed above, taking Advanced Placement classes and passing the AP exams saves you time and money on college courses. It saves time, since you don't have to spend a semester of college time in those classes, and it saves money because you don't have to shell out for those college units. Pile up as many AP credits as you can in high school to ease the financial strain of your freshman year. There are even grants, like the California Governor's Scholarship, that specifically reward high AP scores and high achievement.

Is your student willing to risk his life for a college education? Then consider applying for a military Reserve Officers' Training Corps scholarship. The army, navy, air force, and marines will pay your way for two, three, or four years of college in exchange for military service when you graduate. These are merit-based, not needs-based, scholarships, so if your student is considering this option, make sure he meets the academic requirements.

You can't afford *not* to look into every possible source of funds for college. Keep good records of what you've applied for, keep copies of every application, and keep applying, and you and your student will be well on your way to paying for college.

# The Devil in the Details

Even with everything in place and your student all but sleeping in his new dorm room, you have to check and double-check that the process is still going as planned. In May of Chris's junior year, the Upward Bound program paid for his SATs and any other testing and application fees he needed to complete the process of applying to the University of California system. The following spring, Chris received his letter of acceptance to Davis. Over the summer, all we had to do was prepare for September's classes. Or so we thought.

The first part of August, my intuition suggested that I call to make sure everything was in order at the university. I have learned to listen to my intuition. When I inquired into my son's status at the school, I found out that some essential paperwork was missing from his housing and financial aid files, and that without these papers he was not officially enrolled in the fall. No one thought to call to tell us this; I had to discover it for myself. We made two separate trips that August to fill out paperwork we thought we had completed in May.

A couple of weeks following these incidents, the other shoe dropped when we were told that one of the offices could not find any file on Chris Chandler. All of his paperwork would have to be resubmitted. I was livid. On the final ride to campus, Chris tried to calm me down, asking me not to embarrass him. I shot back with, "I'd better go embarrass someone right now, because you are about to be embarrassed out of a college education." The devil was working overtime. After arriving on campus and being transferred from one person to the next, from the admissions office to the financial aid office to the bursar's office, I finally said to the poor worker behind the teller's window, "We are not filling out one more piece of paper. If his file is not found in the next five minutes, I will go directly to the news media and tell them about all of your measures to keep yet another Black child from getting his education. We have worked his whole life for his college opportunity. We are not leaving here without everything being in order, and I am not coming back, unless it is to help him move in."

It took about twenty minutes to find his file, but I didn't have to go on television to make it happen. It had fallen behind a filing cabinet. I was assured that going to the media was not necessary; everything was in order for his beginning school in two weeks.

I was prepared to wage the same war at the end of the first semester, but to my surprise, I received a phone call from the university admissions office, assuring me that Chris had completed the necessary paperwork for the following semester and everything was ready to go. I was also instructed to please allow Chris to take care of his future arrangements; he was a college student now and should be able to take care of his business on his own. I agreed with that, but I also made it clear that I would not hesitate to intercede again if the situation warranted it. I was not interested in making friends with the folks at the admissions office; my only interest was insuring that Chris, who had worked so hard, be allowed to attend the college of his choice.

# Miss Sharon Says

**Match Your Student to a College:** Identify his needs, strengths, and interests, and explore the widest field of options out there. Despite all your hard work in this area, you might end up choosing wrong. Don't panic. You have not failed. Transfers happen.

**Aim for an Appropriate Degree:** So your student has a C average. Can she still go to college? Yes, but she might need a year or two of community college to show she can do the work.

**Apply for Aid:** Free seminars on filling out the FAFSA paperwork are available to all. Check your public library and community resource center for one near you.

**Assess Various Colleges:** Don't limit your search. Look at all the options with an open mind and, once you have all the facts, start weeding out the top contenders.

**Follow Through:** There is no end to the college process until graduation day. Keep track of deadlines, follow up on paperwork, and check periodically that everything is in order.

# Part 3

## Off to College—and Beyond

College is a big step. You've been talking about it and planning for it for years, but the impact of having your student move out is something you can't really anticipate. You and your student have to prepare emotionally for the separation.

And now that your student has gone to college, what next? You may think your job is over, and in a sense it is. You can stay involved in your student's career, but you need to evaluate your own options and set your own goals. In my Getting on with *Your* Life workshops, I brainstorm with parents about what they want from the rest of their lives now that the kids are on their own. It's time to figure out what *you* want to do—get an education, change your career, start a new business, whatever you choose—and then plan how to make it happen. You will be amazed at how much you have forgotten about living your own life. Without the demands of your kids' schedules, you have time to volunteer somewhere, start your own club, investigate a new job possibility, plan a trip, or return to school yourself.

# Chapter 8

# Yes, Your Student

# *Is* Going to College

The first emotion you might feel when your student moves out and goes to college might be relief. Their childhood is over, you've done your job, they're adults now, you can focus on something else. But then you look around your house, and you miss them. You worry that they're going to be all right. And your student might be feeling lost, alone, and confused. Or elated, energized, and in charge. Most likely, he or she will feel all of these things at different times.

Nurturing our kids when they are out of the nest and on their own continues to be a parenting duty. It's important to let your student know that you are still there for them. My kids have been out of the nest for several years, but we still communicate on a weekly basis, usually by phone, but I like to talk to my kids by mail too. The U.S. Postal Service will, for a mere handful of change, take a piece of paper on which you have written your thoughts and deliver it directly into the hands of the person it is addressed to. I am still amazed that this can happen—it is something we take completely for granted and never seem to fully use. Try it. Try writing a letter and sending it to your student. If you really can't think of much to say, get into the habit of sending a card. They're not just for birthdays. There is nothing quite like the feeling of opening your mailbox and finding, in with the junk and the bills and the catalogs, a real piece of mail to open. But you have to write letters to get letters. So try writing as a way to keep in touch while staying at a distance.

E-mail, of course, is just another way to write a letter. If you and your student are online, either at work or at home, you can set up an easy, friendly, but still-far-enough-away system for keeping in touch. My kids involve me in decisions about their postgraduate educations and about their lives. I'm glad that they still respect my opinions. Sometimes they even follow my advice. And I'm still careful only to offer it when they ask for advice, not before. That's the hardest part. I have to remember that we, the village, have invested years of training to get them to where they currently are: responsible, independent adults. I am reminded of the verse in the Bible that says, "Raise up a child in the way that he should go and he will not stray far from that path." I know they are well on that path, and I have to trust now that I've done enough to put them there. It's their turn to walk it.

That doesn't mean I am not in their life or that I don't care what happens to them. I'm still their mother. It's just that my role has changed. Sometimes that means I am at a distance, and sometimes that means I am right there participating in their daily lives. When we raise our kids to be independent and responsible, whether they attend college or get a job right out of high school, we have fulfilled our parenting obligations. What they do with what you have given them is up to them. We can root for them, be in their corner, be there to listen to them, spend time with them, but we cannot live their lives for them.

## Study Abroad

Sometimes, though, we get to participate. Corey's junior year in college was her exchange program year. After more than two years at college and my constantly encouraging her to spend her weekends on campus participating in activities and making friends, she called me one day and informed me that she was going to South Africa. My first comment was, "OK, I know I wanted you to stop coming home so often, but I didn't mean for you to go to another continent!" My nest now felt truly empty for the first time. Sure, she had been officially gone for a while, and Chris had been gone even longer, but at least they were both within the same time zone. And traveling to Africa was not just a weekend jaunt away, one where she would be back home the following week; she would be all the way around the world from me for six months. I immediately began researching the country by accessing Web sites and purchasing books. I wanted to know if she would be safe. After all, Africa to me then might as well have been another planet, and my baby would be living there.

My emotions were mixed. I was excited for her, but I was also concerned, worried about what might happen. The continent is so turbulent; the indigenous Africans are rebelling and taking back the land and their heritage from the colonials. Civil wars like the ones in the Ivory Coast and Liberia spring up overnight, lasting for decades, and my baby was on her way over to all of that. Cape Town, South Africa, had declared an end to apartheid fewer than seven years before; who knew what the country had in store as far as peace and rebirth were concerned?

When Corey arrived in South Africa, she called me after stepping off the plane and said, "Mom, I'm finally home, I can breathe." That feeling was short-lived, however, as the reality of her situation sank in. Foreign, American, college educated, privileged in so many ways above what the indigenous South Africans would ever experience—she was perceived as arrogant or snooty by Blacks in South Africa. During apartheid, the indigenous people (Blacks) were reminded daily of their lowly place in the world.

South African society is as layered as rock and seemingly just as unchangeable. The Whites in South Africa still comprise only 10 percent of the population. They are the businesspeople, landowners, and until the abolition of apartheid, the politicians. The mixed-race Coloreds are the Blacks who have mixed with Whites or with the major subgroups of Indians or Asians. They live in the apartment complexes, some own homes and businesses. They are the middle classes. The Blacks still do not associate with the Coloreds. Corey was none of these things. She was considered a "coconut"—brown on the outside and white on the inside. The simple action of sitting on the steps at the university, talking with friends and eating her lunch between classes, was seen as uppity by the Black students, just because the students she sat with were White. Once they got to know her, all her strange ways were dismissed as American eccentricities. The Blacks at the market, when they learned she was an American, assumed she was rich and tried to overcharge her for everything she wanted to buy. It took time, and a lot of soul-searching on Corey's part, to come to understand the attitudes, prejudices, and qualities of the people in her adopted country. I experienced her frustrations as well as her joys, all through the magic of e-mail.

I had been concerned about our ability to communicate while she was gone. Long-distance phone calls would have to be few and far between, since charging them to my phone would be too costly and having Corey pay at her end would be worse. Despite our reputation in South Africa, this American was not immensely wealthy. One day while standing in line at the grocery store I spied a phone card for sale. I had never used one, but decided to give it a try. I reasoned that it would limit the amount of time we could talk based on the dollar amount on the card, and I was right. The card was a godsend. I sent one to Corey whenever I could, and I kept one myself. Written letters took a long time to arrive, so we also stayed in touch, on an almost daily basis, by using e-mail. I laugh to think how our long descriptions of daily life here in California and there in Cape Town flew back and forth almost instantly over networks and wires.

*School was OK today. My professor, Chakka, from Tanzania, is disgusted with us because he feels we don't know how to think. He says he is trying to teach robots and we should already have developed reasoning skills.*

*I told him about you and your program, and he invited*
*us to meet with him if you come to visit. Tell everyone*
*hello, I miss you. Will call you on Sunday.*
*Love ya. Corey*

Corey also sent me the astonishing news that I could listen, over the Internet, to the very same local radio stations that she listened to in her dorm in South Africa. I would tune in and listen to the news to keep track of the political climate and reassure myself that Corey was not in danger of being in the middle of an insurrection. The site that presented the radio station also featured African artists and clips from African newspapers. I immersed myself in the same culture that Corey was living in and I felt much closer to her, even though we were in fact still thousands of miles apart.

I confess, Cape Town called to me. I wanted to visit this remarkable place, one that I had only heard of through geography lessons, newspapers, and my daughter's e-mails. If I went now, my room and meals would be provided by Corey's program, I had the time and I missed my baby terribly. I left for Cape Town on my birthday, June 4. It was a terrific birthday present.

Several weeks before Corey was scheduled to return home to the United States, I traveled to Cape Town. I spent two exciting weeks exploring the city and hanging out with college students. I was the resident mom for eighteen students, occasionally cooking and counseling, nightclubbing, and meeting their African classmates at the weekly barbecues. The kids, so far from home, welcomed me as both a parent and a member of their group.

The final hurrah of Corey's trip was a safari in Namibia, Botswana, and Zimbabwe. She camped out in the wild, visited the villages, saw Victoria Falls, and simply drank in the natural beauties of the countryside. When she came back from Africa, she was suddenly off and running. This girl who I couldn't get off my couch in high school was now an accomplished traveler willing to solo on trips near and far. She had immersed herself in the foreign culture and surroundings of Africa and emerged a citizen of the world.

The college experience can open up so many worlds for students and their parents. As I tell my workshoppers whenever I talk about my trip, Corey was as pleased to have me there as I was to be there. Having Corey officially out of the nest made our relationship stronger and put us, in a way, on the same footing as world travelers.

## Back to School—for Yourself

Let's face it: This is the time of your life. Time to put your money where your mouth is. You've been preaching college, college, college for your kids, so maybe it's time you went to college yourself. If you already have a degree, you can go back and get another. College isn't just about one subject. Try something new. Maybe take yourself down a new career path. I remember a parent saying to me, "I can't go back to school because in the three years it'll take to get my degree, I'm gonna turn fifty!" So I asked her, "How old will you be in three years if you *don't* go back to school?" Let's face it, time passes whether you're doing something or not, so you might as well get out there and *do*.

Returning to school was more difficult than I had imagined it would be, but getting a two-year associate's degree in interior design finally allowed me to acquire some formal knowledge of fine art and building design. After completing the classroom requirements for the degree, I then had to perform a sixty-hour internship. Finding the time to study was an exercise in organization skills. Many a time I would spend the night and early morning completing swatch kits, design boards, or writing assignments until 6:00 a.m., then take a short nap and be at work by 8:30 a.m. All the day planners I have handed to my students, all the times I have preached "plan ahead!" to my kids, and there I was, meetings my deadlines at the last possible minute. It was a humbling experience, one that gave me a greater understanding of what college-bound kids really need in order to succeed.

I paid for school through grants and loans, so I didn't have very much to pay back. My janitorial business—the one I had set up so that my kids would qualify for low-income programs—qualified me as well for grants and scholarships to see me through three years of school. Attending school at this time in my life really gave me a great sense of accomplishment. I didn't just finish either; I finished with a 3.5 GPA. This process took three full years. Finding a mentor and finding the time on top of my parenting duties and my full-time job was a challenge, but the reward of my degree was worth it.

Whether you decide to get a degree or not, you can still take classes that broaden your mind and improve your outlook on life. Don't worry that you're going to be "the old fuddy-duddy" on campus either. Adults are returning to school in record numbers. In the last ten years, the number of students over traditional college age rose 13 percent (http://www.ed.gov). About two out of five students on campus are over twenty-five, so you won't be alone. Check with your local colleges to see who has the best support system in place for older students and who offers the best range of continuing education classes.

## Emptying the Nest
## (and Keeping It That Way)

Why are we the only creatures on earth who allow our grown offspring to return to the nest? What is it about our society that thinks it's OK for kids to come and park themselves back in their childhood bedrooms after you think they've left for good? I love my kids, but I made it clear that once they graduated from college they were only welcome in my house on visits. They're not gone out of my life, they're just gone out of my house, and I am enjoying my freedom from my daily involvement in their lives.

I remember that when my nest emptied it was lonely at first. Suddenly I was able to do the things I wanted to do, with only occasional cries for help from my kids, but I didn't know where to begin. I had for years talked about starting a business where I would help parents raise their children with a family goal of a college education. I even toyed around with developing a program. I created a brochure and some business cards. I began surveying people in the community to see if there was a market for my services. At the same time I was still working a full-time job. I was uncomfortable with the idea of quitting my secure income in exchange for an uncertain economic future. I could not take the leap of faith that starting my new business would require. Then fate intervened.

My full-time job as outreach coordinator for Sacramento Neighborhood Housing Services was, according to my doctor, literally going to kill me. The stress and all the attendant physical symptoms were slowly sapping my life away. I recovered slowly, learning over the next two years how to relax and better handle stress. I underwent treatment for depression, and, with my doctor's care, conquered the depression and acquired the ability to move on with my life. Keeping doctor's appointments, dealing with workers' compensation and disability representatives, and occasionally dragging myself out of the house to birthday parties and family activities was all that I could accomplish during that time.

After months of support groups, therapy sessions, and good old-fashioned talks with my mother and my close friends, I finally began feeling better, and I realized that God had closed the door on my former career. Now it was time for me to help Him open a window on my future career. I asked myself what I now ask my workshop participants, "What do you want to do with the next forty years of your life?" I already knew I wanted to continue helping people, especially the parents in my community. It made sense to begin seriously planning my new business.

I decided I needed a short break before I took the plunge into this new phase of my life, so I drove to Reno, Nevada, and checked into a casino hotel and gambled for an evening. In a way, I have always been a gambler, taking risks in my life that I think other people look at as gambles, but I have never been the kind of person to lay money down on a table and risk watching it all disappear. This time, however, I felt like I had an angel on my shoulder. I won a $4,000 jackpot and two $1,000 jackpots in one evening. No one could have been more surprised than I was. I had never won anything before, but I knew enough to get out while I still had it all in my pocket. Driving home, I thought of all of the things I could purchase—a new washer and dryer, landscaping for my property, a new summer wardrobe, living room furniture, even cosmetic surgery—but something in the back of my mind kept saying, "You have to invest in your new business." Yes2Kollege Education Resources, Inc., was born.

## Miss Sharon Says

**Forge Ahead:** Make lists of your dreams, goals, and interests. Take classes. Put in the time to figure out what you want. Don't be dismayed by the process—it may take a while. Use visualization techniques to put yourself in a different career.

**Go Back to College:** Education is never a waste of time. You don't have to become a poet to justify taking a poetry class. Have fun with it!

**Try Something Completely Different:** Whether it's travel or mountain climbing or needlepoint, don't limit yourself to what you already know. Don't worry what someone else thinks about it. This is your chance to put your money where your mouth is and be a lifelong learner yourself.

# College Prepares You for Life

At the end of my workshops I always hand out evaluation forms that I ask the parents to fill out and return. Over the years I've gotten everything on those forms, from "Great class!" to "No comment." One thing that gets repeated over and over, though, is how these parents are going to go home and apply the techniques they've learned to their own family. One woman wrote that she didn't understand before that there is a difference between discipline and punishment. A man enthused over how helpful it had been to exchange information with other parents. He said that the encouragement he felt from the workshop would help him be a better parent and more outspoken in his role as a father. Many parents expressed a wish to take their newfound knowledge and prepare their student for college.

I am so blessed to be able to motivate, energize, and educate parents and students. I am empowering people to become better parents, set family goals, and learn to navigate the educational system and raise college-bound students. The other day, I felt those old negative feelings begin to creep up on me. I started thinking that the business wasn't moving along as fast as I would like and that my financial situation could be a heck of a lot better. A voice in the back of my brain promptly said, "Don't even go there, girlfriend. You are truly blessed. You are living a great life. You own your own business, travel where you like, you're healthy, and your spirit feels free and rejuvenated. And best of all you did an excellent job of raising two beautiful and successful children."

In my vision for the future, Yes2Kollege Education Resources, Inc., will open community learning resource centers for families throughout the country. Each learning center will house a library of college information and resources; offer parenting skills workshops and employment opportunities and training for families and internships for students; and assist students applying for college with financial aid, applications, testing, and career planning.

Mainly, Yes2Kollege centers will provide family enrichment and early college-preparation training programs for parents and college students so they may return to their schools, churches, and community centers with the knowledge to guide their young scholars to college opportunities. One day soon, I hope to be joined by my kids, Chris and Corey, who will take care of, respectively, the center's legal and business concerns and someday step into my shoes as CEOs. Everything starts with a dream. All things are possible.

My nephew Brent and niece Blair have been hearing all their lives about the educational exploits of their cousins Chris and Corey. They were barely walking and talking when Chris went off to college, and they had just started elementary school when Corey left home. My sisters and brothers and mother, along with other family members, have for years listened as I shared my stories about my scholars. Brent and Blair were listening too.

Not too long ago, while overhearing me update the family on where Chris and Corey were in their educational progress, Brent, now eleven, piped up, "Aunt Shay Shay, if Chris is going to be a lawyer and Corey is working on her second master's degree, then Blair and I will have to become doctors in order to pass them up." The precedent has been set. My kids are setting the standard for the next generation of college-bound students.

And my career as a parent is not over. In a way, I feel like I can become the parent of every person who attends my workshops or who reads this book and uses even a little of my method in parenting their own children. We all want to raise successful individuals whose lives will be better and easier than ours. If you set your student on the college-bound path, you help keep them there, and you insist on their respect, you will raise a responsible, hard-working grown-up. Through dedication to these ideas, we can change the world, one student at a time. College is the end of their formal education, but it is just the beginning of a rich and rewarding life. Being successful doesn't always mean being rich in dollars, but it *should* always mean being rich in opportunities and experiences.

I believe that is the most any of us can ask.

# Resources

Online resources are a good first stop for every kind of college-bound research, from financial help to book suggestions to college prep programs. I teach all my parents how to search the Internet, so even if you don't have a computer at home, you can go to the public library and start getting the information you need. The sites listed here are just a tiny taste—you will find so much more on your own using these as starting points.

## College Bound

http://www.ed.gov
U.S. Department of Education
1-800-872-5327

http://www.yesican.gov
http://www.yosipuedo.gov

Bilingual site for Hispanic families looking to make college a reality for their children.

http://www.collegeboard.com/
Register for the SAT, research colleges, and much, much more.

http://www.petersons.com/
Compare colleges, get financial aid info, shop!

http://easnetwork.com/easgrp/Learning/DetailedGlos.html
The Education Association Services provides on this site, among other things, definitions of every term you need to know regarding college and financial aid.

http://guideforparents.com/
An Internet guide for parents of college-bound students.

Family Involvement Partnership for Learning
1-800-USA-LEARN

http://www.parent-teen.com/
A good general site, with great links for the college bound.

## Talking to Teens

http://www.about-teen-depression.com/
Learn how to recognize depression and find out about treatment.

http://www.talkingwithkids.org/
Lists of difficult subjects and how to talk about them, including HIV/AIDS and violence.

http://www.theantidrug.com/ei/conversations.asp
What to say and how to say it about drugs.

http://www.niaaa.nih.gov/publications/makediff.htm
You can download a booklet about talking to teens about alcohol.

http://www.ehow.com/how_18819_talk-child-about.html
Step-by-step instructions on topics to cover when talking to your teen about sex.

## Special Education

http://www.seriweb.com/
A clearinghouse of special ed information links.

http://www.nichcy.org/
Information on children with disabilities of all kinds.

## Career Exploration

Here's a list of summer as well as school-year programs that encourage students to investigate science and mathematics career paths and consider their own interests and strengths in new and exciting ways.

http://upwardbound.ucdavis.edu/
Many universities offer an Upward Bound program, but I'm including UC Davis's as an example. Check with your high school counseling office for the UB program closest to you.

http://www.discoverengineering.org
Who invented the snowboard? An engineer.

http://www.eweek.org
National Engineers Week sponsors Introduce a Girl to Engineering Day.

http://www.tryscience.org
More than four hundred science and technology centers have collaborated on this interactive site. Visit science centers around the globe without ever leaving your seat!

http://www.jets.org
The Junior Engineering Technical Society offers programs for high school students. Teams design projects and compete regionally and nationally.

http://www.futurecity.org
Teams of seventh- and eight-grade students work with real engineers to design future cities. Use SimCity to build and research a scale model. Compete with other teams—win a trip to Washington, D.C.!

http://www.engineeringk12.org/students/
Find out more about what it takes to be an engineer, and why math and science are important whether a student chooses to be an engineer or not.

http://mesa.ucop.edu/home.html
California Mathematics Engineering Science Achievement (MESA) homepage.

http://www.jhuapl.edu/mesa/content.htm
Maryland Mathematics Engineering Science Achievement (MESA) homepage. MESA is a statewide precollege program designed to encourage underrepresented populations in the fields of science and mathematics. Find one in your state.

## Reading

http://www.ala.org/
The American Library Association's Outstanding Books for the College Bound and Lifelong Learners is a good place to start if you're looking for suggestions on what to read.

Lists of great books (like the one from http://www.collegeboard-.com in chapter 3) and lists of reading for the college bound (http://www.sms.org/books_co.htm and http://als.lib.wi.us/) are also helpful to print out and carry with you to the library.

And if you're reading along with your student, you can go to http://www.bookwolf.com for book notes (similar to

CliffsNotes) and lists of prepared questions to ask, answer, and discuss. Your student will think you are a deep-thinking genius, able to ask pertinent questions helping him write better book reports that flesh out characters and storylines.

## College Financing Calculators

http://www.collegeboard.com/article/0,,6-29-0-401,00.html
A step-by-step process for determining exactly how much college will cost. Click on:

Expected Family Contribution (EFC) Calculator
College Cost Calculator
College Savings Calculator
Student Loan Calculator
Parent Debt Calculator
Parent Loan Repayment Calculator

## Savings

http://www.upromise.com/
Use the power of your shopping dollars to jump-start your student's college savings. Register the credit or debit cards you use to purchase groceries, gas, and online services, then every time you purchase particular brands, those companies kick money into your student's college fund. The Upromise site also provides other advice for the college bound.

http://www.savingforcollege.com/
Free information about 529 savings plans: what they are, how to set them up, and why you should. Paid services are also available.

---

# Financial Aid

---

http://www.fafsa.ed.gov
Free Application for Federal Student Aid: Serious step-by-step instructions for beginning, continuing, and succeeding at obtaining financial aid.

http://www.edfund.org
EdFund: Low-interest loans and financial management advice. Check out their publication, Credit for College (pub. no. I-110).

http://www.loans4students.org/
Chela Education Financing: Not only do they provide step-by-step instructions for people looking for financial aid loans, in some cases they provide the loans themselves.

http://www.fastweb.com
Search on FastWeb for more than five hundred thousand private sector sources of financial aid.

More!
http://www.finaid.org
http://www.collegenet.com
http://www.fastaid.com

# Scholarship Opportunities

http://apps.collegeboard.com/cbsearch_ss/welcome.jsp
http://www.college-scholarships.com/
http://www.collegescholarships.com/
http://www.scholarships.com/
http://www.collegedata.com/
http://money.cnn.com/

http://startsomething.target.com/
A program through Target stores and the Tiger Woods Foundation, Start Something helps kids set goals and work to meet them. It offers scholarships to kids who participate.

These sites all offer dozens if not hundreds and even thousands of different scholarship opportunities. For scholarships targeted at specific groups (like would-be engineers, budding scientists, and premeds), search the Web for the words *college, scholarship,* and the category of your choice. You'll get lists of corporations and private organizations that offer scholarships large and small in their field of expertise. Beware of any sites that want to charge you money for their search services. You can get this stuff free.

# Military Options

http://www.armyrotc.com/
U.S. Army ROTC.

http://www.afrotc.com/
U.S. Air Force ROTC.

http://www.navy.com/nrotc
U.S. Naval and Marines ROTC.

# About the Authors

**Sharon Chandler** is the founder and president of Yes2Kollege Education Resources, Inc., a nonprofit organization that provides educational workshops and seminars for parents, school groups, civic clubs, and businesses on the importance of college preparation. Y2K's stated purpose is to encourage parents and students to pursue education beyond high school and to instill in students an appreciation for the value of education.

All of Chandler's wide-ranging professional experiences have utilized her excellent communications and public relations skills. For two years, she produced and hosted the television talk show *Rapport,* a monthly community affairs program aimed at the African American population of a large midwestern region. *Rapport* reached an audience of more than two hundred thousand viewers with interviews of local personalities as well as celebrity interviews with entertainers like Bill Cosby and political figures like Shirley Chisholm.

For six years she also acted as news reporter for an ABC affiliate. She covered stories on agriculture, schools, community interest, county and city government, and social service agencies.

As well as working in television, Chandler has worked in various positions:

- public relations for a police department

- executive director of the East Side Human Resources Center, the largest Black-owned and -operated business in St. Joseph, and its only woman director

- executive director of the Northwest Missouri Chapter of the March of Dimes

- founder of a local chapter of a national housing program

- member of the League of Women Voters and a lobbyist for that organization

- business owner

- community organizer

Chandler trains hundreds of parents and students each year on how to become successful students who aspire to higher education. She has contracted with school districts, community centers, parent organizations, government agencies, and nonprofits as a teacher, guest speaker, lecturer, and meeting facilitator. In the past year, she ran classes that reached more than a thousand parents as well as presenting four different workshops in two different school districts. In June 2005, she ran a two-day intensive staff development training for foster care professionals in Chicago, IL. In May 2003, she was asked to return as a guest speaker at the College: Making It Happen program at San Joaquin Delta College, a University of California, Davis–sponsored college information workshop.

She is a certified Child Protective Services Parent Educator for court-mandated classes in Sacramento, California, and a consultant through the On Track Program services with the California Department of Alcohol and Drug Programs. She is currently working as a consultant for a mentoring and alcohol/drug counseling program. Groups such as the Sacramento Unified School District, California State University Hayward, and the Oakland Unified School District have commissioned her Y2K presentations. She has the relevant experience of sending herself back to school as an adult, putting herself through an associate's degree program while her own children were in high school and college, and getting her own children into the colleges of their choice.

Her son, Chris, is a graduate of UC Davis and is attending the University of San Diego School of Law. Her daughter, Corey, is a graduate of St. Mary's College, has her master's degree in sociology from Purdue University, and a master's in education administration at Loyola University in Chicago. She has been accepted into the PhD program at Johns Hopkins University in Baltimore.

**Elizabeth Crane** is a graduate of the University of Pennsylvania with honors in English. After college, she worked as a donor development associate for the Rockefeller University in New York, and then for a financial services firm. After moving to San Francisco, her writing career began at a computer and business magazine, and over the next ten years her work has

appeared in magazines such as *Parenting, Bay Area Parent, HipMama, Woman's Day,* and *conceive,* with business stories in *PC World, Smart Business, Working Woman,* and *University Business.*

Her book coauthored with Richard Raucci *Yahooligans! Way Cool Web Sites* was used as a tool for teaching students how to use and enjoy the Internet. Her essay, "Do Toy Guns Teach Violence?" first appeared in *Brain, Child* magazine and was selected for use in a Bedford/St. Martin's textbook for non-American students learning about American culture and social mores, *America Now: Short Readings from Recent Periodicals.*

She is currently a contributing editor at *District Administration,* a national magazine for education professionals, and a member of the American Society of Journalists and Authors (ASJA). She is also an officer in the ASJA Northern California Chapter.

She is the daughter of a college biology professor and a high school history teacher. Her two sons are in public elementary and middle schools, and they are well aware that they are expected to go to college.